Praise for *Let's Talk*

'We're not currently in the golden era of conversation – it has either eroded away into emojis or escalated into online wildfires. Nihal is a master of the art of conversation, one of the country's finest and smartest interviewers, and his book is both brilliant and necessary. Read this fascinating book and you'll become a better listener, a better conversationalist and better company'

Adam Kay, author of *This is Going to Hurt*

'A brilliant book on the art of conversation. This isn't some half-hearted celeb effort . . . a very impassioned defence of conversation as an art and one of the things that can save and retain our humanity in a world of GIFs and emojis and fifteen second digital dopamine hits. Nihal writes as well as he chats and this book is great'

Matt Haig, author of *The Midnight Library*

'Nihal is nothing less than the most intelligent interviewer in British broadcasting, so I had high expectations for his book on conversations, and it doesn't disappoint. It's clever, original, surprising and reading it made me appreciate why he is so good at what he does – he actually listens to the people he consults. A compulsory book for these divided times'

Sathnam Sanghera, author of *Empireland*

'Nihal hits the nail on the head – again, and again, and again. Breaking news: conversation isn't shouting at a crowd on social media. Nihal has rediscovered the art and we are all winners as a result. A terrific book from a terrific broadcaster. Worryingly good'

Jeremy Vine, author of *What I Learnt*

'Your willingness to ask a question and genuinely listen and converse, as opposed to trying to "win" the argument, is just so refreshing. An insightful, important read'

Stacey Dooley, author of *Are you really OK?*

'If ever a book needed writing it was this one, now. Fascinating and thought-provoking'

Jane Fallon, author of *Faking Friends*

'Brilliant in the ear and just as brilliant on the page. To read him is to get a lesson from a master practitioner of the art'   Anita Anand, author of *The Patient Assassin*

'The conversation king'

Laura Whitmore, author of *No One Can Change Your Life Except For You*

'There is no more important task today than improving the conversations we all have. And there is nobody better to guide us than Nihal Arthanayake'

Matthew d'Ancona, author of *Post Truth*

Nihal Arthanayake

Let's Talk

How to Have Better Conversations

TRAPEZE

First published in Great Britain in 2022 by Trapeze
this paperback edition published in 2023 by Trapeze,
an imprint of The Orion Publishing Group Ltd
Carmelite House, 50 Victoria Embankment
London EC4Y 0DZ

An Hachette UK Company

7 9 10 8

ISBN (Mass Market Paperback) 978 1 3987 0224 0
ISBN (eBook) 978 1 3987 0225 7
ISBN (Audio) 978 1 3987 0226 4

Typeset by Input Data Services Ltd, Somerset

Printed and bound in Great Britain by Clays Ltd, Elcograf S.p.A.

www.orionbooks.co.uk

*For Mrs Rohini Arthanayake, Mr Tilak Arthanayake.
Eesha, Aarya and Kingsley. All my amazing friends
whose conversational skills uplift and inspire me.*

CONTENTS

INTRODUCTION

I have written this book for a simple reason. I want
you to understand why it is important that we have
better conversations, to unpack exactly what I mean by
'better conversations' and to equip you with the tools
to start having them. Before we begin, let me dispel any
doubts you might have that this book has nothing of
value to pass on to you by asking four straightforward
questions.

1) Do you tend to communicate more through digital means (FaceTime, Microsoft Teams, Zoom,
   WhatsApp, email, etc.) than by talking to someone
   in person?
2) How many times in the last month have you been
   distracted by your phone when someone is trying to
   talk to you?
3) In the last five conversations you have had, how

much of what the other person said can you remember?

4) Do you avoid having difficult conversations?

If you felt a pang of guilt answering any of the above, then *Let's Talk* is the defibrillator you need to revive your ability to connect, rather than purely project. It would be a great idea for us all to spend some time thinking about how we really engage with the people in our lives – how much time we spend listening to them and interacting with what they express to us. We all, of course, excuse our lack of engagement by pleading that we are increasingly time-poor. Why should we hold a proper conversation if such a thing can be abbreviated and digitised for greater efficiency? Who needs emotions when emojis will suffice?

And yet, if you have taken a moment for reflection, I think you will have wondered what has happened to public, and even private, discourse in recent years, considered how reductive and divisive conversations have become. This is not how it has to be. We must attempt to recalibrate ourselves to understand and value just how important moments of conversational connection are. If the pace of life, the distractions of technology, the demands on our time and the pressures we put ourselves under are collectively undermining our ability to be in the moment with each other, then we have to do something about that. This book is the beginning of that conversation.

As this is a book about dialogues, I should first allow you the opportunity to ask me a question, and quite a fundamental one at that: what qualifies me to write this book? I am not an academic, as the C, D and E that I underachieved in my A levels will attest. The degree I eventually ended up doing was in history and English literature.* I have no qualifications in the scientific fields. You will not find hundreds of references at the end of this book stacked up in order to impress you,† nor peer-reviewed papers written by me swirling around in the academic ether. What I do undoubtedly have in my corner is the fact that I am a multi-award-winning broadcaster who has been having the most extraordinarily wide array of conversations for twenty years.‡ To give you a sense of the breadth of my conversational endeavours, I shall spend the next few moments name-dropping like a person desperate to get a table at the hottest restaurant in town.

I have spent many an hour in the company of some of the greatest minds and entertainers of our age, including assorted winners of the Booker Prize, BRIT Awards, Grammys and Oscars, and those who have had Pulitzer Prizes and BAFTAs bestowed upon them for their sterling work. At any given moment during my allotted three hours a day on national radio, a listener could be sitting

---

* If you ever feel the unquenchable need to find out more about the childhood of James VI of Scotland, I am your man.
† OK, there are some references.
‡ This doesn't automatically qualify me to demand so much of your time, but it does prove that when it comes to the art of having a conversation, I am in the Premier League of conversationalists.

transfixed as they listen to the likes of Hollywood film star Matthew McConaughey talk about the volatility of his parents' relationship, or to the gripping life story of Collette, a former sex worker and drug addict, who at one point had her children taken away from her and has since managed to turn her life around completely. For the past two decades, I have been paid to do this, but the roots of my interest predate a BBC contract – more on that shortly.

Talking to people has always come naturally to me. Even when I joined BBC Radio 1 in October 2002 as a specialist music DJ and then went into the world of speech broadcasting via the BBC Asian Network, I never really regarded what I did as in any way unusual, nor did I attempt to analyse the importance of this ability. I was just having a conversation. Tucked away on my living-room bookshelves are two Sony Gold Awards (the pinnacle for any broadcaster), a BBC Radio and Music Award for Interview of the Year, a British Podcast Award, an Amnesty International UK Media Award and a plethora of Asian Media Awards. To add to that, I was also inducted into the Radio Academy's Hall of Fame while still in my forties. The point of listing all of these achievements is not to self-aggrandise but to illustrate the fact that even though I have received the acknowledgement of my peers for as long as I can remember, what I do for a living has never seemed unique or needing further introspection.

My lack of self-analysis changed when I joined BBC 5 Live in September 2016. It was a much bigger station with a much larger audience than I was used to. It was also a febrile time across the UK. The acrimonious and divisive Brexit vote had taken place in June of that year and the majority of those who stepped into the ballot box had voted to leave the European Union. We were also just months away from the hugely controversial election of Donald J. Trump as the forty-fifth president of the United States of America. It was, as I remember it, a time of division and rancour as views hardened and consensus was hard to find as people picked sides and resolutely stuck to them. People on the right used the term 'identity politics' to disparage a set of beliefs, and there were those on the left who were too keen to brand people as racists for having an opposing view. Across the political spectrum, everybody was engaged in allowing their politics and their identity to become inextricably linked. And woe betide if a person expressed views from the 'other side'. The social media companies had a field day as their algorithms herded us into our own little thought enclaves and everyone manned the barricades of their fortified opinions. And there I was, a man with a microphone, a platform and an overwhelming unease at what I saw as a transformation from civility in public and private discourse to one of enmity, outrage and suspicion.

Those early months gave me a window into a world where it seemed that everyone's default setting was to transmit their views and nobody wanted to give space to anyone with opposing ones. Prior to the ruptures of the EU referendum, I had previously relished the chance to host verbal pugilists slugging it out with each other, but after 2016, I really didn't want any part of it. That type of broadcasting is designed to be a dopamine hit meant for viral videos and shareable GIFs. So, rather than hosting preordained battles between people simply adopting contradictory positions for the sake of having a row, I looked to have longer, more meaningful conversations with interesting people who were willing to share their experiences with my new and bigger audience. During that time, what kept being fed back to me from listeners, and what certainly helped grow my confidence, was how much they appreciated a presenter who actually listened to his guests' answers, thought deeply about the questions asked and allowed the conversation to flow freely without the strictures of a pre-written script. This book is in part my attempt to understand what I do, seemingly without thinking, for twelve hours a week on national radio and, in doing so, impart those learnings to you.

Flash forward to the present day, post-pandemic and ensuing lockdowns, and much is made of the damaging consequences of living our lives through those rectangular devices that consume so much of our time. On a Saturday in January 2022, when sale signs were plastered across every shop window, my daughter and I walked through the food court of a gigantic shopping mall on the hunt for a free table. What I began to notice was how many people were looking at their phone screens as someone was talking to them. The sight of a couple transfixed not with each other but with a handheld piece of technology saddened me. I wondered how invested in these moments, supposedly of connection, these people actually were. For most of us, tech is not a substitute for companionship; its promise of connectivity is a mirage, leaving us potentially lonelier. We know that loneliness is such a concern that in October 2018, then Prime Minister Theresa May appointed a Minister for Loneliness. The British government even launched a campaign in the summer of 2021, with an accompanying hashtag #LetsTalkLoneliness, whose two top recommendations were to check in with a neighbour and to keep in touch with family, friends and neighbours. It was an unprecedented sign of how disconnected from each other we had become that the then Prime Minister saw fit to launch a cross-government strategy to get to grips with the problem of loneliness in our society. In the literature that accompanied the launch, the Government stated that around 200,000 older people in the UK had not had a conversation with a friend or relative in over a month. Allied to this was the acknowledgement that there were both mental and physical health implications connected to loneliness, such as Alzheimer's, heart disease and depression.

For *Let's Talk*, I wanted to find out how important conversations are to a range of different people. While I hope I have now justified what qualifies me to write authoritatively on this subject, what makes this book a unique proposition is that I have used my interviewing skills and the connections I have made to seek out conversational experts. These individuals have spent much of their adult lives striving to perfect how they communicate with colleagues, friends, family, patients, the vulnerable and even their enemies. In the following pages, we will meet a lawyer turned politician, a hostage negotiator, a documentary film-maker, a famous TV presenter, a captain of industry, a historian, a number of professors and a former Olympic table tennis champion turned bestselling author.

In Part 1, we will amble through the history of conversation in order to truly understand why we are now at a tipping point with regard to the future of public and private discourse. In Part 2, we will delve into the mechanics of what could help us to be so much better at talking and listening. In Part 3, we will encounter extraordinary people whose words have meant the difference between life and death. In Part 4, we will commute to the office to discuss conversations in the workplace. And, finally, in Part 5, we will journey from the television studio to the therapist's chair and I will direct my lens of inquiry towards those whose job it is to speak for a living.

There are real-world applications to all the conversations in this book. After reading it, I hope you will perhaps be able to find a way back from a family estrangement, walk away from a toxic relationship and into a better one, find commonality after a racist altercation, or even manage to build a bridge following a falling-out over religion. For me, conversation is a vocation, but for you, this could be the book you need to give you the confidence to speak and – more importantly – develop the skills to listen. I hope that in reading the coming pages you will understand why this matters to me and why it should to you.

Before we dive in, I alluded to the fact earlier that it wasn't the BBC that taught me how to be a conversationalist. It was my mother, Rohini Nimal Arthanayake. She was a nurse in the NHS for nearly forty years. What she brought home with her from that hospital every weekend was an appreciation of how much humans needed to connect when at their most vulnerable. People who had been looked after by my mum and her dedicated colleagues never forgot it. Walking through Harlow town centre was like accompanying someone running for president as they made their way through their party's convention after a barnstorming speech. Black, white, old, young, conservatively attired or in a tracksuit, my mother would always give them the time of day, listen intently, respond accordingly and move onto the next fan in the queue. That ability to connect with other human beings no matter their background certainly has rubbed off on me. She showed me the beauty and connection to be found in the deepest or briefest of exchanges and how much stronger it is to listen than it is to occupy space purely with the sound of your own voice.

My mother also showed me the value in relating to others on a human level, devoid of snobbery and judgement. Even though her own childhood was mostly bereft of kindness, she never failed to display warmth and empathy in nearly all of her interactions, apart from when my brother and I were being a right royal pain in the arse. This is another reason as to why I am writing this book, as a homage to my mother. I believe that we all have it within us to be conversationalists and to understand that if we are all to co-exist peacefully, and scupper the plans of those who would rather we didn't, then it all begins with people talking to each other. So, let's talk.

PART I

THE EVOLUTION OF CONVERSATION

I

Let's Talk About History

The Oxford English Dictionary defines 'conversation' as 'an informal talk involving a small group of people or only two'. Interestingly, this sense of communicating with someone only took hold in the English language in the late sixteenth century. While the following definitions are now obsolete in modern English, the etymological roots of the word saw conversation defined as either a 'place where one lives or dwells' or as a synonym for sexual intercourse, referring to *criminal conversation*, a legal term for adultery in the late eighteenth century. So as not to mislead you about the tone of this book, I won't be following this line of inquiry any further.* What is more dif-

---

* However, for anyone interested in this subject, please see my follow-up book, aptly named after the hit song by the American hip-hop trio Salt-N-Pepa: *Let's Talk About Sex*.

ficult is to pin down precisely when the first conversation occurred. Such an endeavour is akin to trying to work out why all your previous relationships failed. Yes, there is information out there, but the further back you go, the more muddled it becomes. And to stretch the comparison even further, nobody can agree on who dumped whom. So you can continue to query the origins of the break-up all you want, but it is unlikely you'll ever get a definitive answer. This is where we stand with the beginnings of vocal communication. In order to try to approximate this, we have to understand when language itself began to develop and for what purpose. So without getting bogged down in too much conjecture, let's home in on two possible start dates.

To employ social media speak, on one side of the language development debate reigns the intellectually superior #TeamHomoSapiens (which translates as Team Wise Man). This school of thought proposes that language only really came into existence with the arrival of our human ancestors anywhere between 300,000 and 50,000 years ago. With their bigger brains and larger chins, Homo sapiens had the neurological, biological and evolutionary machinery to rise above the elementary basics of communication and begin the process of human progress that we reap the benefits of today. There are, of course, murmurings of discontent at the back of the class by another group of academics backing the alternative theory, which involves our long-gone ancestor #TeamHomoErectus (which means Team Upright Man). They propose that language began to develop nearly two million years ago. The justification for this far older hypothesis can be found in Professor Daniel Everett's 2017 book *How Language Began*. Professor Everett spent four decades among the Pirahã people of the Amazon developing theories on linguistics.

One of the tenets of this claim rests on the fact that Homo erectus fossils have been found in various far-flung parts of the world, from the island of Flores in Indonesia to an island in the Arabian Sea and also on Crete. How could they have ended up in different parts of the world without the construction of rudimentary rafts to get them across distances too far to swim? Constructing a sea-worthy vessel, as you are no doubt aware, requires collaboration. In order to be able to work together to build a boat, there must have been a way of communicating that involved language, as assembling a rickety raft went beyond crudely gesticulating to each other. As the world grew relatively more sophisticated, mere hand signalling could not deliver.

Professor Everett's work also contains a takedown of the man who is sometimes regarded to be the father of modern linguistics, Noam Chomsky, who believes that humans are born with the instinct to create language. Professor Everett maintains that language is, in fact, something that we learn through the culture we grow up in and that then in turn helps the culture to evolve, meaning that language is not innate in all of us from birth. At a TEDx lecture that he gave in 2017 in San Francisco, Professor Everett called language the greatest technological discovery ever made and waxed lyrical about it being the foundation for all technologies that have come since. Rather than believing language to be the exclusive preserve of Homo sapiens, he makes a compelling argument for us to look much further back into history for its origins.

The alternative hypothesis that language originated with Homo sapiens went largely unchallenged for over five decades. It's called LDT, which stands for laryngeal descent theory, and was proposed by an American cognitive scientist called Philip Lieberman in 1969. The basis of this theory is the idea that in order to make the vowel sounds 'a', 'i' and 'u', which feature in every language on Earth, the larynx had to descend from the third cervical vertebrae in the neck, where it is in monkeys, to the fifth one, and voila – you can employ those three vital vowel sounds to say 'Backbiting butthead!' at whoever you wish to. However, in 2019, a multidisciplinary group of scientists that included human palaeontologists, primatologists and experts in infant cognition concluded that focusing on the larynx as the sole driver of vowel pronunciation was a bit of a red herring and that monkeys were able to make these sounds well over twenty-five million years ago. This seems to have annoyed Mr Lieberman, who called the latest research 'a complete misrepresentation of the entire field'.

The major problem with attempting to pinpoint when and where language originated is that all of the fleshy biological apparatus that comes together to make verbal communication possible decomposes. Where there is flesh, there is likely to be little or no fossilised remains to refer to in times of confusion. So, rather than becoming bogged down in the murky backwaters of our primate ancestry, it is worth usually pole-vaulting over quite a few epochs to land in a period when societies began to value the power of discourse and revel in the opportunities and entertainment those who were proficient in it provided.

Language and speech evolved and became more sophisticated as more complex societies required a greater breadth of words to communicate within their own circles and also with other communities. Historically speaking, the chance to show off through debate and discourse has captivated the upper and middle classes for as long as there has been a social construct called class. Two and a half thousand years ago in ancient Athens, the agora, or marketplace, would have been abuzz with the conversations of rich Athenians engaged in trading, philosophising or catching up on the politics of the day. As the sun set, the wealthy men would gather for a night of decadence at a symposium, which literally translates as 'drinking together'. At these liver-degrading events of aristocratic debauchery, the symposiasts (the name given to those who attended a symposium) would chug down copious amounts of wine as musicians and acrobats performed around them. In Ancient Greece, aristocratic men fully appreciated the need for enlightening conversation. The variety performance included the very speakers themselves, who were picked to enhance any social event with a *bon mot* or a provocative question acting as an axle about which the conversation smoothly turned. If you were lucky enough to be invited to one of these events, it probably meant that you were rich and erudite.

In the late 360s BCE, the Greek historian and mercenary Xenophon wrote *Symposium*, a record of the conversations that took place one evening between a wealthy Athenian named Callias and a motley crew of the comfortable sandal-wearing denizens of Ancient Greece, including none other than Socrates himself. As the evening wore on and the guests were exposed to a variety of entertaining acts, Socrates declared, 'These people, gentlemen, show their competence to give us pleasure, and yet we, I am sure, think ourselves considerably superior to them. Will it not be to our shame, therefore, if we do not make even an attempt, while here together, to be of some service or to give some pleasure one to another.' This, of course, was not the Greek equivalent of car keys in a fishbowl (that would probably come a bit later on in the evening). This was Socrates laying down the conversational gauntlet. He went on to address the host of the evening directly: 'I should like to have Callias redeem his promise; for he said, you remember, that if we would take dinner with him, he would give us an exhibition of his profundity.' What follows is an exhibition of the Greek philosopher's stock-in-trade Socratic method of drawing out ideas by challenging each other's given positions on any given subject.

Reading *Symposium* by Xenophon (not to be confused

with the better-known *Symposium* by Plato), you are drawn into a world that is designed to verbally go high and low, to pit one wit against another and to make sure no man – because only men were invited – is spared having his words dissected by his peers. It is safe to say that silence was not an option in such esteemed company. A point Socrates picks up on when addressing another one of the guests present. 'Hermogenes, could you define "convivial unpleasantness" for us?' he asks, and so begins the back-and-forth. 'I do not know; but I am willing to tell you what I think it is,' Hermogenes replies. 'My definition of "convivial unpleasantness" is the annoying of one's companions at their drink.' With Socrates as the engine that powered the conversational element of the night, each attendee was then asked to recount what aspect of their lives they were most proud of. As each man answered in turn, others would interject respectfully once a natural pause took place, but never rudely interrupt, and prod the conversation forward, so that it was a constantly rolling series of points, counterpoints and witty observations.

The account of this intellectual jousting of Ancient Greece's high-born men was written by a man who claims to have been at this raucous dinner party, although historians believe that he would have been too young to have attended when the gathering actually took place in the year 400 BCE. It is not a verbatim recording as we would know it today, but it does demonstrate what the Greeks regarded as the heights that conversation could reach. *Symposium* describes a gathering of men who were intent on politely teasing each other, using conversation as a means to exercise their intellect and display for all present the heights to which their minds could soar through the mastery of conversation, rather than simply exhibit the trappings of the social class to which they mostly belonged. To read it is to be drawn back into antiquity and the grandstanding of men who view conversation as a performance art, but also to realise how invigorating good conversation is – not because of an overall need for consensus but for testing each other's opinions. In Ancient Greece, good conversation was every bit as important as good wine – although what effect the latter had on the former, we can only surmise.

Over a millennia after Socrates entered the home of Callias, and divided by 2,000 miles of land and sea, a simple conversation used as an aid to teach apprentice monks Latin provides us with the first recorded example of a conversation taking place in English, or Old English to be precise. Titled *Colloquy*, which translates as 'conversation', it was between a Benedictine abbot, Aelfric of Eynsham, who lived from c.950–1010 in Oxfordshire, and a motley crew of students from lower- and middle-class professions. The young men – a fisherman, a merchant, a hunter, a cook, a salter, a baker, a carpenter, a blacksmith, a ploughman, a lawyer and a shepherd – had gathered together because they wished to be educated and attain a degree of intellectual social mobility through mastering Latin. Their social class is important to note because this is also one of the earliest examples of people from such diverse backgrounds having their lives recorded for posterity, a rarity in Old English literature.

There seems to be no lack of self-awareness in how bereft they are of the tools needed to be a conversational heavyweight in the Middle Ages. They collectively state, 'We want to be wise.' They implore in unison to their teacher to give them the tools to be able to 'speak properly and with a wide vocabulary for we are ignorant and badly spoken'. The teacher replies, 'How would you like to speak?' And, aware of their own shortcomings, those in attendance reply, 'We want to speak correctly and with meaning, and not with meaningless base words.' Such was the desperation of these young men to be wise, they were willing to endure physical punishment in order to attain it. 'Would you beat us and make us learn? For it is better for us to be beaten to learn than to remain ignorant.' They were literally asking for it. Thankfully, throughout the course of the discourse, the rod is left unused.

The conversation consists of a back-and-forth between the good abbot and the young men in his company. They outline their professions and a verbal competition takes place in which each argues why they are the most important component of the society they inhabit. The teacher asks provocatively, 'What can we say about you, cook? Do we have any need of your skills?' The cook responds defiantly, 'If you drive me away from your community you would eat your vegetables raw, and your meat rare.' The baker is then asked to justify his role, to which he graphically replies, 'Without bread all your food would become vomit.' Which is a bit of a stretch, even for tenth-century England.

As the dialogue develops, the young men grow in confidence, with the teacher pushing them further and, on occasion, them pushing back with a robustness that shows Aelfric is open to being challenged himself. Out of the blue, the teacher asks a boy, 'Have you been beaten today?' The young man responds immediately, 'No, I haven't since I behaved cautiously.' The teacher presses on: 'What about your friends?' And, perhaps presumably knowing that even in medieval England the thoroughly modern term 'snitches end up in ditches' was appropriate, the boy responds, 'Why do you ask me that? For, I dare not reveal our secrets to you. Each one of us knows if he has been beaten or not.'

A thousand years after these dialogues took place, the humour, candour and macho posturing of these boys shine through. The teacher asks, 'What did you have to drink?' and 'Boy', as he is simply referred to in the text, replies, 'I drink ale, usually, if I drink at all, and water if I have no ale.' Not a particularly healthy take on hydration. The teacher wants to know more. 'Don't you drink wine?' And the boy's class and status become all too apparent in his answer: 'No, I am not rich enough to be able to buy myself wine: Wine is not a drink for boys or fools but for old men and wise men.' Such insights fascinate me as you discover so much of these young men's lives. The hardship of ploughing the land in all weathers or the responsibility of protecting the sheep from wolves. A young hunter boasts about cutting a boar's throat as it ran towards him, which impresses the abbot no end.

Colloquy shows us how important it was for these boys to learn how to communicate effectively, giving them a modicum of social status that in their middle- to lower-class professions they would not otherwise achieve, however much they promoted the invaluable nature of the roles they played in Anglo-Saxon society. What begins as a standard question-and-answer session becomes a rapid interplay between the different professions present. In this dialogue, like the one in ancient Athens, the participants want to impress with words. While the men in Ancient Greece were largely engaged in social aggrandisement through exhibitions of wit and wisdom, these individuals in medieval England from far lower on the social spectrum simply wanted to be educated in order to elevate them from the daily grind of their tough lives. Towards the end of *Colloquy*, the teacher inquires of the boys, 'I ask you why are you so keen to learn?' To which they reply, 'We do not want to be as the wild beasts who know of nothing but grass and water.'

Throughout history, verbal communication has been the bedrock of advancement, the exploring and explaining of ideas and a means to understand each other better. From the collaborative construction of a raft that is deemed sturdy enough to make a potentially fatal crossing hundreds of thousands of years ago, we then travel forward to a dinner party just over two millennia ago that was set ablaze by a gang of sparkling speakers. From there, we propel ourselves a thousand years to tenth-century England and a group of boys simply appreciating the power of education. For as far back as time will allow us to see, conversation has played a vital role in our collective development.

2

Henry Hitchings:
The Growth of Conversation

Hold my hand as we are about to take a gigantic 700-year leap through history to the coffee houses of eighteenth-century London. We'll encounter a burgeoning culture that distinguished itself by the ability of people to keep a room enthralled by their awe-inspiring conversational skills and also through the idea of conversation as a way of challenging others' views.

In 1709, the Irish writer, playwright and politician Sir Richard Steele wrote in *The Tatler*, a publication he helped create, that the definition of a gentleman was 'a man of conversation'. For those that we would now refer to as the urban middle classes, a conversation was a chance to shine intellectually, proving that you were abreast of all the latest ideas in the fields of science, politics, literature and philosophy. By calling the periodical he co-founded *The Tatler*, Sir Richard was quite possibly taking a misogynistic dig at what he deemed the idle utterances of women, the tittle-tattle of small talk, which was conceived to be inferior to the intellectually robust style of dialogue he championed. Although it is certainly worth noting that men were also accused of tattling at the time. Sir Richard wrote extensively about the dos and don'ts of conversation. 'A man that stammers,' he once wrote, 'if he has understanding, is to be attended to with patience and good-nature; but he that speaks more than he needs, has no right to such an indulgence.' I wonder what he would have made of the barrage of monologues that takes place on social media.

At the turn of the century, *The Tatler* was part of an explosion of printed material that hitherto had been too expensive for the common man to get his hands on. Pamphlets, periodicals and solitary sheets of paper known as handbills provided exactly the jumping-off point needed for a wider stratum of society to start discussing the issues of the day in the largely alcohol-free coffee shops that were springing up across London.

The seismic social, political and scientific changes that were afoot throughout this extraordinary century led cumulatively to the ascendancy of the art of conversation. Today, over a billion people speak English globally, making it the most widely spoken language in the world, so I wanted to examine a period in British history when this language was given a reverence that was felt beyond a Royal Court or a playwright's pen. It is in this era that the concept of conversation as an art form is given centre stage to a much wider audience.

In the London of the latter half of the seventeenth century, the artistic icon of stimulating dialogue was Dr Samuel Johnson. Some of his contemporary detractors would have argued that his conversation was largely one-sided and combative. He nevertheless revelled in the benefits that 'honest' conversation could bestow on both speaker and listener. Writing in *The Rambler*, a twice weekly periodical, in December 1750, Dr Johnson claimed that 'It is scarcely possible to pass an hour in honest conversation, without being able, when we rise from it, to please ourselves with having given or received some advantages.'

In order to truly understand this moment in time, I enlisted the expert knowledge of the author and historian Henry Hitchings. After attending Christ Church, Oxford, and then completing his PhD on Samuel Johnson at University College London, Henry went on to publish the award-winning *Dr Johnson's Dictionary* in 2005. He is a warm, incredibly affable and enthusiastic exponent of Samuel Johnson's Herculean feat of compiling an English dictionary over 250 years ago.

We started our chat by taking a look at the era in which Dr Johnson lived and the converging forces that gave rise to a flourishing conversational scene. Alongside a more economically viable way of printing and distributing literature, places where the newly fashionable beverage of coffee, rather than alcohol, was being consumed were opening up to allow people to discuss the words contained within these new magazines and newspapers. The absence of intoxicating liquor meant that the conversation was expected to be of a higher quality than that found in taverns and alehouses of eighteenth-century London. Surprisingly, perhaps, Henry also mentioned the impact of the introduction of street lighting in the eighteenth century. Where once people would have remained in their homes rather than venture out into the dark with all its constituent terrors, the Londoners of the eighteenth century were keen to find places to hang out in away from their lodgings. As well as you now being able to see a robber approaching you, the formation of the precursor of the modern police force around 1750 would have also aided the proliferation of coffee houses and clubs across London as people felt safer than ever before. A city of 650,000 people could now embrace the night in a way that only the rich in their horse-drawn carriages could have dreamed of doing before street lights. Combine all of these seemingly unrelated elements together and you can see how a burgeoning conversational movement thrived. For the first time, middle- and upper-class people mixed in spaces created for the express pursuit of engaging conversation.

'There's this incredible flowering of conversation and it's facilitated by all these things that happen at the same time,' explained Henry. Dialogue was expected to be instructional, inspiring and informative. It was, as Henry pointed out, 'an engine of social mobility, but also a product of it'. The new periodicals like *The Tatler* helped develop and popularise the rules of polite behaviour, including in conversation. What is worth noting here is that politeness and conversation were inextricably linked and, as Henry says, 'the idea of politeness is a hot idea in the eighteenth century.' Beside the precondition of civility, there was also an emphasis on disagreement. 'One really important idea in the eighteenth century, an idea we find quite difficult now, is that disagreement is a good thing. You have to have a collision of opinions, which results in a new opinion,' Henry said, before immediately decrying how social media has turned a difference of opinion into an excuse to call each other names, rather than asking, 'Why do you think that?'

In the twenty-first century, across the UK, there is a stereotype of the rude Londoner with whom it is impossible to strike up a conversation. The scenario is of a commuter minding his or her own business on the London Underground who recoils in terror as some chirpy person from the north of England attempts to engage in an unsolicited exchange of pleasantries. It wasn't always so, as Henry described: 'One of the key points in the eighteenth century is that conversations were with strangers, whereas now we see conversation as something we have with our friends and family.'

I asked him to talk more about what he thought the main differences are between how eighteenth-century Londoners regarded conversation and how we see it today. 'We find the idea that the art of conversation is something that you could cultivate by reading about it, by studying other people's conversation, quite weird.' He then remarked upon the decline in the number of clubs that were primarily used as places to congregate and talk to each other. 'There were all sorts of clubs and neutral spaces – not just grand clubs but political clubs, social clubs, clubs for people who shared a niche interest, such as flowers or philosophy. The space for them has been squeezed by the demands of work and by family.' He ended on a downbeat note, as he said somewhat forlornly, 'Those were places for the flourishing of conversation.'

In 1700, a play called *The Way of the World* by William Congreve premiered at Lincoln's Inn Fields in London. In it, one of the characters asks, 'Is there a worse disease than the conversation of fools?' This prompted me to ask Henry whether the purpose of conversation three centuries ago was to be inspired and whether that had changed? 'That was the ideal people had,' he replied. So what does Henry believe to be many people's idea of what a conversation is today? In answering this question, his ire was reserved for that daily occurrence most people who work in an office environment have to endure. 'The meeting is, for a lot of people in the twenty-first century, a paradigm of what conversation is, and yet, the meeting is one of the lowest forms of civilisation, and is the enemy of thought and listening and getting anything done.' While I would disagree with the blanket dismissal of meetings per se, I am sure we can all remember an occasion whereby everyone present left the meeting thinking, 'Well, that's forty-five minutes I will never get back.'

Of course, in the twenty-first century, the physical meeting place, the various clubs that provided neutral ground for conversation of many types, has been largely replaced by the digital one of social media. That is a very different sort of proposition and one in which many of the social rules enthusiastically expounded by Richard Steele and his contemporaries are thought not to apply. As Henry reflected: 'So often, the Twitter conversation is two monologues rather than a real engagement. Part of a real engagement is the breathing space to let what someone said sit with you before you have to retort. I think the conversation of fools is one where there is no breathing space.'

3

Johann Hari:
Conversation and the Attention Crisis

As I was reading Johann Hari's bestselling book *Stolen Focus*, I was shocked by how relevant to me much of what he had written about was. In the book, the writer and journalist somewhat ironically focuses his forensic gaze on the subject of our seemingly diminishing attention spans. As someone who was finding it increasingly difficult to fix my concentration on a single task at hand, the book was both timely, terrifying and liberating. I then wondered if there was a correlation between what Johann was addressing and my own concerns about the diminishing importance of conversation in our daily lives.

At the start of our meeting, he immediately acknowledged how his work and my worries are entwined. What began as a forty-five-minute window in our diaries to flesh out the similarities turned into a two-hour conversation. Throughout the course of it, Johann effortlessly danced from reciting a personal anecdote to quoting an academic study. He covered monumental moments of social change and intimate moments of personal reflection. His energy was energising and illuminating and I knew within seconds that his inclusion in *Let's Talk* was going to be revelatory.

'They're intimately connected,' he began. 'Conversation is one of the most precious forms of attention that humans have.' He did not hold back from using the word 'crisis' to describe what was happening to our attention spans and what was happening to our ability to engage in conversation. He cited work carried out by the cognitive neuroscientist Professor Michael Posner at the University of Oregon, which, in Johann's own words, described how long it took to get our thoughts back on track after being impeded by a distraction: 'If you're interrupted, it takes you on average twenty-three minutes to get back to the same level of focus that you had before you were interrupted. So, if in the middle of a conversation, you stop and check your text messages, it takes you twenty-three minutes to get back to the level of focus you had before.'

How often have you been on the receiving end of this or have allowed yourself to be distracted? Could you actually part company with your phone by placing it on silent and out of sight while conversing with another human being? Or would you succumb to the psychological condition known as nomophobia, where you fear the very thought of having to be separated from your mobile? We will be introduced later on in the book to the work of Professor Sherry Turkle, but it's worth referencing her now for the phenomenon she calls 'being alone together', whereby we think we're having conversation but we're actually just alone with our devices. Johann unpacked this idea further, saying, 'It causes a deterioration in the quality of the attention that you bring, which in turn makes the conversation less good, which in turn means conversation itself seems less appealing because it's not giving you the thing you need, which is being seen. Throughout virtually the entire stretch of human history, there has been no single device that has had such a detrimental effect on our ability to pay attention to each other.'

Johann then introduced into this maelstrom the issue of narcissism, which he described as 'attention getting trapped in your own ego'. Again, it is a phenomenon that he believes is on the rise. As an example to illustrate a wider point, he told me that during a sojourn in the picturesque New England town of Providence, Massachusetts, he was in a small café 'pretending to read *David Copperfield* but in reality attempting to eavesdrop on people'. In walked two men who Johann quickly ascertained had met on a dating app and were meeting face-to-face for the first time. Over the course of two hours, these two men didn't respond to a single thing the other one said. Two monologues were occurring in place of one dialogue. In this bizarre scenario, the most extreme example of this lack of active listening was when one of the men said that his brother had recently died and the other simply maintained a narcissistic soliloquy without skipping a beat.

As we look to the future, how can we combat this rise in narcissism that is being exacerbated, according to Johann, by being 'immersed in machinery like Facebook and Instagram, where everyone appears to be talking about you. I think that increases egotistical behaviour, which decreases the possibility of conversation'? There are solutions to these challenges and academics have been hard at work trying to figure them out. Johann points to the work of Professor Raymond A. Mar, who, alongside Professors Keith Oakley and Jordan B. Peterson, published a paper in 2009 called 'Exploring the link between reading fiction and empathy'. This was a follow-up to a piece of research that had dealt with this subject matter three years before. Professor Mar saw reading fiction as a 'kind of empathy gym', to use Johann's description, and his experiments showed how those who read fiction could spot certain signals in a way that was different to those who primarily read non-fiction. In a test that is usually used to diagnose autism, people were shown images of the area around a person's eyes and asked if they could ascertain how that person was feeling at the time the picture was taken. The more fiction someone read, the better they were at deciphering how that person felt when the camera took a picture of their eyes.

Continuing the discussion of what he felt was the inextricable link between attention and conversation, Johann established the importance of sleep in helping us to stay focused. According to him, 'We sleep an hour less than we did in 1942. Children sleep eighty-five minutes less than they did a century ago.' If you are someone who finds it difficult to sleep, the next statistic that Johann recited to me isn't going to make you feel any better. 'If you stay awake for nineteen hours, your attention is as bad as if you've got legally drunk.' Johann also highlighted the importance of having a healthy diet that doesn't produce huge energy crashes and energy spikes: 'At the moment, we eat a diet that causes our energy to spike and crash all the time. Having a diet that doesn't do that, that releases energy steadily throughout the day, improves your attention and will improve your ability to have a conversation.'

In the previous chapter, Henry Hitchings and I discussed the challenges of persuading people that conversational skills can be learned. For Johann Hari, it all came down to the work of the American psychologist and professor of psychology at Stanford University Carol Dweck, who coined the terms 'fixed mindset' and 'growth mindset'. Simply put, if you believe that you cannot be better at having conversations, then you are firmly encamped in the fixed mindset school of human growth and development, which states you are what you are and no amount of work will change that. The alternative to this rather defeatist personality trait is the growth mindset that encourages you to believe that hard work, persistence and good teaching will allow you to be better at talking and listening to your fellow humans. The fact that you have read this far into the book means that you are already exhibiting quite encouraging signs that you are of the growth mindset grouping in society, but that may also mean I am preaching to the converted.

One of the aspects of dialogue that Johann is most

passionate about is the willingness to take part in conversations with people whose views differ from your own. In this regard, he has a lot in common with the patrons of the coffee houses of eighteenth-century London. After writing a book about addiction, called *Chasing the Scream*, Johann was contacted by a woman who was a Republican-voting evangelical Christian from Mississippi. This person was vehemently anti-abortion and rather than just voice her disapproval robustly, she fostered a lot of children, most of whom were born to parents who had severe addiction issues. She reached out to Johann after reading his book accepting that automatically criminalising addicts was not an effective way to address the problem. Johann, a self-described 'left-wing, gay atheist', wouldn't have ordinarily found himself becoming friends with a woman whose views were so diametrically opposed to his own. But, over the course of time, that is what happened.

As well as being a charming anecdote, it proves that conversations build bridges between people who on paper you would never believe could stand to be in the same room as each other, let alone find common ground or become good friends. He went on to say, 'Connection is far more transformative than contempt. Conversation is a form of connection, right? Conversations with people who don't agree with you is a form of respect. If we can't have conversations, what hope can we have?' Johann paraphrased a quote by former president Ronald Reagan, which loosely goes 'my 80 per cent friend is not my 20 per cent enemy', to highlight the increasingly tribalised world we now live in, in which 'our 99 per cent friend is [now] our 1 per cent enemy'. To explain what this means: as the forces of polarising political and social issues swirl around us every day, the demand that we 'pick a side' and refuse to engage with those deemed to be on the 'other side' of the debate grows louder. Accepting that people do not agree on everything, and respecting that, is a way of achieving greater connection and less contempt in society. That percentage part of their views that isn't aligned to your own should not prevent you from finding any commonality whatsoever.

Johann concluded our thoroughly illuminating conversation by telling me about the often celebrated and sometimes maligned journalist Andrew Sullivan, who wrote a groundbreaking essay for *New Republic* magazine in 1989. The cover story put forward 'The Case for Gay Marriage', which back then was a concept so outlandish that even large sections of the gay community could not accept its premise, let alone the Democratic and Republican establishments in America who united in their opposition to it. Seven years later, in 1996, Democrat President Bill Clinton signed into law the Defense of Marriage Act, defining marriage as 'the union of one man and one woman'. Two years before that, Andrew had moved to Provincetown, New England, to die. He was HIV-positive and expected that his life would be cut short by AIDS, a disease that had taken so many people he had known, so with the remaining time he believed he had left, he wrote a book in which he expanded upon the idea of gay marriage. Called *Virtually Normal*, it was published in 1995 and Andrew never expected to live long enough to see if anyone cared about it, let alone one of its provocations actually becoming law. But Andrew did live and that book, based on that essay, ended up being quoted by the US Supreme Court when, in 2015, the highest court in the land ruled that the fourteenth Amendment of the US Constitution required all states to grant same-sex marriages and recognise those that had taken place in other states.

The reason that Johann told me this story is because of what it says about the power of connection, of reaching out to those who are politically opposed to you and finding a way to cover the impasse. 'When I feel depressed about the possibility of progress, I always imagine going back in time to Provincetown in 1994 and saying to Andrew, "OK, Andrew, you're not going to believe me but ..."' By this point, he was evangelising about the greatness and power of conversations even more than I was and we finished our very own chat with Johann summing up the core of why it is important that we talk to each other: 'Because that's what it means to be alive.'

The evolution of conversation throughout history provides ample examples of how progress manifests when people devote time, energy and resources to speaking with each other. I hope that the openness required to welcome different opinions into your life isn't being slowly diminished and that we see conversation as a tool for expanding our minds, viewpoints and experiences. History is scarred by inhumanity but it is also uplifted by dialogue, which has seen sworn enemies make peace and human invention and creativity flourish through collaboration.

PART 2

THE MECHANICS OF A CONVERSATION

4

Let's Talk About Talking

What constitutes a really good conversation? Must such an exchange involve declarations of love? Or is it defined by two people playing banter tennis interspersed with chest-bursting moments of hilarity? Or must a really good conversation be made up solely of awe-inspiring examples of oratory? The answer is all of the above or none of the examples given. What defines a high-quality exchange of words is open to interpretation by those partaking in it. Whether you have been summoned into your boss's office and come away from the meeting feeling inspired and stimulated or you are seated alone in the back of a taxi after a first date with a warm sense of happiness cascading through you, the brain is processing these moments and chemical reactions are taking place that will affect how you feel and how you think. A significant social interaction may be an interplay that lasts less than a minute, such as a barista commenting on the coolness of your name as they scribble it down on your disposable coffee cup. A melee of hugging and jumping around following a match-winning goal, the euphoria resulting in a conversation between two supporters who had been strangers just moments before, who share this moment of joy with each other, pumped up on endorphins. Long or short, loud or quiet, emotional or transactional, amiable or angry, conversations take many different forms.

In order to understand how we can get to a better place, it is useful to be able to recognise what is going on in our heads when we have good and bad conversations – or what those who analyse such interactions would prefer to call effective and less effective ones. What is the hormone produced as a smile breaks through, a bond of trust is created or a moment of joy is sparked by another's words? Is there a universal structure that forms the tree trunk of any conversation, and are all the dialogues that take place just differently sized branches that sprout from one single great, immovable edifice? In the domain of neurological inquiry, scientists have delved deep into that fleshy super-computer that is the supreme commander of our mind, body and soul to uncover the neural processes that click into action when we speak to each other, and what in turn they produce.

This chapter will attempt to understand what science can tell us about the benefits of having a good conversation. At this juncture, I should remind you that *Let's Talk* is as much a journey into subjects hitherto unknown to me as it may well be for you. I hope you'll find the insight provided by my expert interviewees and the work of those who have devoted years of academic study to exploring these areas as illuminating as I did. Their studies look at the outcomes of different scenarios on the quality of social interactions we have, and their findings show why it is important for our mental health that we become better at verbally communicating with each other and realise the value of doing so more often.

You may have noticed lately that the couples all around you in restaurants are just doomscrolling their way through their dinner dates. In all directions, millennials and generation Zers are frenetically jabbing at the blue light of their phone screens like moths headbutting a porch light, while children retreat further into the addictive world of online gaming and fifteen-second-long dance moves. As the encroachment of technological advancements threatens to engulf us, I'm sure many of you have yearned to go back to a time when social media meant sharing your newspaper with a stranger and a troll was still just a mythical creature from Norse folklore. This was an era where posting meant sending a physical letter and only birds tweeted.

Over the decades since computers first emerged and then conversely shrank in size as their capabilities grew, there has been a plethora of research exploring the role that conversation plays in our lives. Academics have investigated, for example, whether small talk has any beneficial role in our social interactions, or if there are any psychological and biological ramifications for those who have fewer and poorer conversations. They have conducted studies to assess how the quality of our interactions has changed as technology has advanced – not because they are anti-technology or anti-progress, but because they want to understand how the machine and the human mind can co-exist.

Investigations into how technology can recalibrate human behaviours predate the smartphones we hold in our hands today by almost forty years. In 1984, ten years before IBM launched the SPC, widely considered to be the first smartphone, Sherry Turkle, professor of the social studies of science and technology at the Massachusetts Institute of Technology (MIT), wrote a book called *The Second Self: Computers and the Human Spirit* that explored how computers were affecting our psychological and emotional states. When she arrived at MIT in the late seventies, this self-confessed humanist found herself amid people who spoke about the human mind using the technical language that accompanied the brave new world of computing. By using this lexicon, they were replacing physiological terminology with the technical terms more applicable to a hard drive than a human brain. Some of her students spoke of acts of interacting with machines as among the most emotional ones of their lives. In the course of working with computers, these academic encounters began to change how the humans, who spent so much time with the machines, viewed and interacted with other people, and even how they saw themselves. Professor Turkle's book featured interviews with nearly 400 people, from schoolchildren to university students and those engaged in the fields of computing and artificial intelligence. She wanted to look at this new-ish world of computing through the lens of humanism, psychology and anthropology to reveal how these technologies would shape our behaviours.

We shall hear more about Professor Turkle's extraordinarily prescient work later on. Suffice to say, you do not need people in lab coats to tell you how it feels to have positive human connections in your life. You already recognise the warmth that surrounds you after a friend has made you laugh, a colleague or boss has praised your work or a partner has said that they love you. But do you know what the long-term effects are of having more of these connections in your life, as well as the consequences of having very few of them? These conversations release a hormone in the brain that we should all have more of in our lives called oxytocin – remember the name because I will be talking more about what some call the 'cuddle hormone' and others the 'love hormone' shortly.

There is no doubt in the minds of academics and researchers that having more positive social interactions leads to increases in self-esteem, well-being and overall psychological and physical health. In a study entitled 'Social Relationships and Depression', three researchers looked at how different social interactions in the participants' lives affected the likelihood of depression developing over a ten-year period. They predicted that by 2030 'major depressive disorder' (MDD) was set to have the biggest impact on disease globally, so it was of prime importance that the possible drivers for depression emerging in someone's mind were examined. Their findings were unequivocal, stating that, across a variety of different social connections, the poorer your core social relationships, the higher the risk of experiencing depression ten years later. People who had the highest-quality relationships with friends and family were half as likely to suffer with depression than those with the poorest bonds with the people in their social and familial circles. Put another way, the academics estimated that one in seven adults who had the lowest-quality social relationships would suffer from depression years later, but only one in fifteen would be affected by this debilitating mental health condition if they had the most meaningful and rewarding friendships and relationships with their families. Interestingly, their work didn't find a link between the frequency of those interactions and the impact on mental health. It seems that it is quality and not necessarily quantity of time spent nurturing and enjoying these relationships that matters. One of the really useful conclusions of this study is for the global gatekeepers of health policy because the data recommends that public health officials and practitioners build questions about the quality of social relationships into the diagnostic process.

For those languishing at the bottom of the heap when it comes to strong social bonds with their families and communities, the news gets even worse. Research published in 1979 looked at 7,000 adults in Alameda County, California in 1965 and then followed up with them nine years later. For those with the fewest social ties to friends, family and community, their risk of dying prematurely was twice that of those who happened to have the most engagement with the above groupings. Another aspect of this area of research is the importance of what sociologists would call 'social support'. This relates to the emotional value of having high-quality relationships in our lives and how these support our mental health and in turn reduce the risk of us falling foul of certain physical health conditions, such as heart disease and even certain cancers.

If we were made more aware of the science that explains the benefits of in-person-to-person communication, then perhaps more people around the world would joyously embrace the life-enhancing effects of spending more quality time in each other's company. Imagine if after every 9 a.m. meeting, your boss said, 'OK, everyone, your thirty-minute chat time starts now,' and just left everyone to talk to each other. Wouldn't it be helpful if your NHS app pinged you an alert every fortnight that reminded you about the profitability of in-person contact with a friend or family member? For some reason, that level of realisation and acceptance hasn't become the norm yet. Human contact matters and while it is not always possible to meet face-to-face or carve out time to interact away from our screens, we owe it to ourselves to prioritise seeing our fellow humans in a worthwhile context.

The Community Life Survey conducted by the UK government's Office for National Statistics in 2018 found that young people in England aged between 16 and 24 were most likely to report feeling lonely, with 10 per cent of them saying that they experienced these feelings of loneliness 'often or always'. In the same survey, but conducted for the years 2020/1, which covered pandemic lockdowns, approximately three million people in England felt lonely 'often/always', with the 16–24 age group yet again reporting the highest levels of loneliness.

In February 2022, the Making Caring Common Project, from the Harvard Graduate School of Education, published a report entitled 'Loneliness in America: How the Pandemic Has Deepened an Epidemic and What We Can Do About It.' This new research showed that 36 per cent of all Americans felt 'serious loneliness' and, again, the age group most likely to feel lonely were young adults, with 61 per cent of them expressing these feelings. On both sides of the Atlantic, it was the digital natives, those for whom connectivity is greater than any previous generation in history, who reported feelings of loneliness more than any other grouping. Once we take this lack of connection and add to it research concerning our diminishing attention spans, increased lack of focus and obsession with self, it would suggest that we are in need of a stop-and-reflect moment.

The current trajectory of how we communicate is not fixed. We have it within our control to recognise and develop the skills needed to be able to converse in a more mutually beneficial way. Over the coming pages, you will find further scientifically informed reasons for why we must strive to have better conversations with those we love, those we like and even those we've just met. Although, in order to do that, we firstly need to look up from our phones. Next time you are out in a public space surrounded by crowds of people, take a few moments to see if you can notice how engaged people are with one another. It seems so common for many, me included, to be distracted by the world beyond the person sitting right in front of us. Could this inexorable slide away from the physical realm and into the virtual one be our collective destiny? No, not if you realise what the separation away from each other means – and not just from an anecdotal perspective, but from a scientific one, also. What do you think is happening to the quality of your social interactions when you sit down with family or friends and you all take out your phones and place them on the table?

Back in 2015, the year before Instagram Stories and TikTok launched, Professor Sherry Turkle wrote her fourth book, *Reclaiming Conversation: The Power of Talk in a Digital Age*. In almost every interview she did around the publication of the book, she spoke of research which said that 89 per cent of Americans took out their phones at their last social get-together. She also quoted data that said 80 per cent of Americans believed that act of surrender to our tech overlords (my words, not hers) had an effect on the quality of the conversation they were having, and not a positive one. So even when there was a realisation that the appearance of a phone would denigrate the quality of conversation when meeting socially, people carried on regardless, and yet the general population and media outlets didn't seem to be alarmed by that information.

In July 2012, two academics from the University of Essex published the snappily titled research paper 'Can you connect with me now? How the presence of mobile communication technology influences face-to-face conversation quality'. As long as a decade ago, when the two researchers in question, Andrew K. Przybylski and Netta Weinstein, published their work, there were questions about what effects our devices were having on in-person human interaction. It is also worth noting that back in 2012, those devices had nowhere near the distracting power of today's semiconductor-infused, data-gorging supercomputers. Przybylski and Weinstein wanted to discover what the consequences were for the depth and quality of a conversation if a mobile phone was placed in the vicinity of two strangers when they were talking to each other. For the purposes of the research, one conversation was designed to be a 'moderately intimate topic' about something interesting that had happened to them in the previous month, and the other to be more casual, meaning that neither participant was required to reveal much about themselves. The interesting part was that the phone would not be visible to the participants, but both were aware it was there.

A group of strangers were split into pairs and each sat down to have a chat. For one set of pairs, a mobile phone was placed on an adjacent desk, which was close but not in either's direct eyeline. The other pairs who were engaged in a chat had a good old-fashioned notebook placed in a similar position – just out of vision, but, like the mobile, they were aware of its presence. The two people were then given just ten minutes to talk to each other about something that had happened to them in the previous month – this was designed to be the more meaningful conversation. The researchers then measured a number of things, including if the participants felt that there would be a likelihood of them becoming friends with their opposite number if they were to spend more time in each other's company and whether one of the pair felt a reduction in feelings of empathy and trust. The researchers concluded that 'the mere presence of mobile communication technology might interfere with human relationship formation.' Speaking to those who took part in the study afterwards, the researchers noticed that the effects 'might happen outside of conscious awareness'. Meaning that the phone's presence alone subconsciously informed those present that there was a wider social network that they had access to beyond the confines of the conversation that they were involved in. This had a degrading effect on the dialogue.

What the findings tell us about the effect a seemingly innocuous piece of technology could have on our ability to connect with each other in a meaningful way is quite startling. The people who spent ten minutes having a conversation with a mobile phone present did indeed feel less of a connection with the other person. Just the awareness of it being there prevented the conversational duo from building bonds of trust, empathy and connection, with each party believing the other to be less understanding. Whereas those who had what was deemed to be more meaningful conversation, based around the same initial inquiry but with knowledge of a notebook being nearby, were able to build closer bonds of relatability with each other. It is also important to note that where the conversation was deemed to be more causal in nature, the mobile phone had less of an effect on the participants.

What this suggests is that if you are intending to have a deeper conversation with someone, then the ability to do that will be restricted by having your mobile to hand, ready to interrupt your supposedly important catch-up. As Professor Turkle points out, our acquiescence to this omnipresent piece of kit is tantamount to telling your lunch partner that there's only so much attention that you can give them because your email, Instagram and Twitter alerts are on a par with whatever it is they have to say. You have in essence told your speaking partner that you are prepared to be constantly interrupted by your phone through the course of your time together.

It has been widely reported that both Bill Gates and Steve Jobs limited the amount of time their children spent on devices, with Gates' children not laying their hands on their own smartphones until they reached fourteen, and even then phones were banned from the table when the family gathered to eat.

If you have ever heard someone say 'you're never alone with a phone,' ask them to define what 'alone' means to them and how much genuine joy they are deriving from swiping on a screen. The fact is that the connectivity that you believe is broadening your world via your Wi-Fi or 5G is not going to be anywhere near as fulfilling as the connection made with the people who are sat right in front of you. At the risk of labouring the point, the avail-ability of information at your fingertips is not analogous to the enrichment that comes with shared instances of authentic human attachment. The fleeting dopamine hit of a social media like or follow is no replacement for a heart-to-heart with a friend over a bottle of wine.

While many billions are being spent in tech company research and development labs making the hardware, and more importantly the apps that exist within their shiny shells ever more addictive, we are still masters of our own destinies so do not have to meekly consent to retreating further from each other and deeper into the universe that exists once our fingers meet our touchscreen. It is neither accidental or coincidental that we are finding it increasingly difficult to extricate ourselves from our mobiles. They are intentionally addictive, inviting you to a virtual world of enhanced sociability. Each app installed uses tools such as the abundance of pop-up notifications which draw you in and keep you hooked. Our brains experience a different chemical reaction when we substitute a touchpad for an opportunity to talk.

This brings me back to the neuroscience of conversation, specifically what is going on in a region of the brain known as the hypothalamus. This is the tiny pea-sized part of the brain that sits just above the pituitary gland and, among many other things, regulates our emotional responses. It may constitute less than 1 per cent of the human brain's total weight, but what it lacks in size, it certainly makes up for in complexity and importance. It is this area of the brain that regulates our emotional responses and releases our hormones, including oxytocin (not to be confused with the infamous opioid OxyContin, which brought the misery of addiction into the lives of millions of Americans). The hypothalamus stimulates the pituitary gland to release oxytocin into the bloodstream. There are a number of jobs attributed to this handy little hormone, so please allow me to run you through a few of them.

Oxytocin is a vital component of childbirth, helping the muscles in the uterus to contract, and can even be administered to help speed up a long drawn-out labour. Once the baby has arrived, oxytocin then sets to work getting the breast milk from the milk-making glands in the breasts, via another bout of muscle contraction. Once the milk hits the ducts, they also tighten up in order to get that wholesome breast milk from the nipple into the baby's mouth, and hopefully what follows is some rest for both mother and child, post-breastfeed. The production of this hormone becomes in tune with the mother's own reactions as she sees, hears or touches her newborn. Even thinking lovingly about her baby can produce oxytocin. It ultimately helps with the bonding process between infant and mother.

As I mentioned before, oxytocin is sometimes nick-named the 'love hormone' as it is produced when some-one finds themselves being turned on by another human and even has a role to play when we fall in love. And this doesn't just mean romantic love – oxytocin helps us to build bonds of trust and empathy when having posi-tive conversations with each other. Lower levels of this so-called 'cuddle hormone' have been linked to anxiety and depression, so making sure we boost the amount of oxytocin in our bloodstream is no bad thing. So if there is a deficit, then how can we go from the red into the black?

There are several ways that we can get the hypo-thalamus working overtime in the production of this hormone: stretching out your elasticated self on a yoga mat, becoming hypnotised by your own breathing while meditating, dancing to the music you love or having some play time with your dog. But what I want to focus on is, unsurprisingly, the effect that having a really good conversation has on oxytocin production. The very act of listening intently, maintaining eye contact and casting aside unnecessary distractions while communicating with someone increases oxytocin and can reduce levels of cortisol – another hormone, whose presence in the bloodstream is an indicator of stress. For those who prefer texting to talking, be warned – the science indicates that in a stressful situation, if you want less cortisol in your life and more oxytocin, then writing a message with predictive text and pressing send is no substitute for talking it through.

Over a decade ago, three academics from the departments of psychology and anthropology at the University of Wisconsin–Madison and one from the Wisconsin National Primate Research Center wrote a paper entitled 'Instant messages vs speech: hormones and why we still need to hear each other'. The researchers enlisted the services of sixty-eight girls aged between seven-and-a-half and twelve years of age, and their mothers, to look at how speech affects hormone levels. The girls undertook verbal and maths tests in front of an audience, watching dispassionately. As you can imagine, the environment increased levels of stress in most of the participants. After the tests were completed, the children were randomly placed in four different situations. The first group of children were allowed full contact with their parent, which included touch, smell and conversation. The second group were left alone, with no parental contact whatsoever. The third set of children were allowed to speak to their parent on the phone and the fourth batch allowed to only communicate through an instant-messaging programme set up on computers. Afterwards, the amounts of cortisol (the hormone produced in stressful situations) in the children's saliva and the levels of the hormone oxytocin in their urine were measured. Perhaps unsurprisingly, the children who had no contact with their parent and those who only used the instant-message programme saw levels of cortisol rise from a measurement taken before the study, whereas the children who had full contact and those who had only verbal interactions with their parent experienced a decrease in their cortisol levels. Similarly, for the children who got a chance to speak to their parent, whether in person or over the phone, levels of oxytocin rose.

In the closing paragraph to the conclusion of the study, the researchers commented that, even though instant messaging was an effective way of sending information to one another and it was clearly a normalised way of communicating for young people, 'in terms of stress mediation and OT [oxytocin] release, instant messaging was no substitute for spoken language or direct interpersonal interaction.' They made it clear that these results related directly to the interplay between mothers and daughters, but it is not difficult to see how these findings indicate that speech and human contact trumps using text to connect.

Now, why is this decade-old research relevant to the content of this book? It reinforces the idea that there is no replacement for the comforting and bonding experience that comes with talking to someone, especially someone that you trust. These were children in a laboratory environment within the confines of a thoroughly well-planned and executed experiment, so some may ask if it's really possible to build a wider argument based on this study, which would be a valid question. In response, I would say that we have now lived for some time in a world where we rely on texts, emails, WhatsApp and direct messaging to communicate with each other. These modes of communication, although useful, and in some cases vital, should not be allowed to relegate the hormonal benefits of speaking to the people in our lives. These conversations can help to alleviate some of the drama from stressful predicaments and increase levels of a hormone that is fundamental for the building of trust and empathy. Speaking to each other has benefits beyond the exchange of gossip, sharing of experiences or providing guidance. If we pay attention to the person with whom we are speaking, avoid unnecessary conflict and invest time in our relationships, the production of oxytocin and the lower levels of cortisol in our bloodstream will help to prevent some of the darker aspects of the human mind from taking over, such as depression and anxiety, where those suffering with these debilitating conditions have higher levels of cortisol in their bloodstream. We will not eradicate cortisol entirely, of course, as though its nickname 'the stress hormone' makes it sound undesirable, it plays a vital role in preparing the mind and body to deal with physical and emotional difficulties.

5

Professor Elizabeth Stokoe:
The Structure of a Conversation

Elizabeth Stokoe is a professor of social interaction at Loughborough University and has co-written a number of books, including *Talk: The Science of Conversation*, *Conversation and Gender* and *Crisis Talk: Negotiating with individuals in Crisis*. As she has a PhD in psychology and conversation analysis and various academic postings in the behavioural and social sciences, it should come as no surprise that I wanted to interview Professor Stokoe for this book.

I started by asking her why the subject of conversation fascinated her. She enthusiastically replied, 'Who isn't fascinated by earwigging brilliant and sometimes totally mundane conversations?' This became more than just having her attention drawn by a couple having a very public falling-out or an indiscreet friend sharing the scandalous details of a convoluted love life within earshot. What began as any normal person's interest in the lives of others evolved into a working life that has involved the analysis of everything 'from people on first dates to police interrogations of violent suspects'.

Professor Stokoe became interested in the construction and deconstruction of a dialogue, the turn-taking, the agendas and the objectives playing out as to what both parties to a conversation hoped to achieve. But also that very first moment, 'the initiating action', that may be non-verbal. A conversation can start before a single word has been exchanged, be it a knock on the door, appearance in a Zoom or 'someone just selecting you with their eyes'. Regardless of the context, where the conversation is taking place or the medium it is being conducted in, her mind is programmed to see beyond the words being said and to look at the mechanics of the very exchange itself.

Professor Stokoe brought up the example of a now infamous exchange that she had seen on TV the previous day between a notoriously combative breakfast TV interviewer and a rather hapless former health secretary. As the two men spoke – one a journalist holding power to account while trying to make headlines and the other a politician attempting to survive the exchange while avoiding headlines – she was fascinated by the structure that underpinned the verbal jousting. From my own perspective, this spectacle was not a conversation but rather an interrogation. I asked the Professor if there was a difference from her point of view. She explained that categorising exchanges as conversational or confrontational is not a useful binary. 'I would see every interaction between humans as "conversational", although we adjust what we say, word by word, to be, say, formal, informal or interrogative.' She picked up on my use of the word 'interrogation' and began to define behaviours that would be associated with that word, such as the persistent asking of the same question while refusing to accept the answers given, which, as she pointed out, could also veer into the territory of harassment.

She cautioned me against labelling and pointed me towards a universal structure that conversation analysts have demonstrated in their research. 'Almost all social interaction,' began Professor Stokoe 'no matter what the purpose of it, has a machinery, so I have many analogies.' The one that she reached for immediately was that of a coat hanger. For Professor Stokoe, what is of primary interest is what is making the social interaction possible. What lies beneath the words being said to ensure that the communication is effective. There may be different types and sizes of clothes that are placed upon it, but the hanger robustly remains the same. Professor Stokoe listed the elements that help form the constituent parts of the coat hanger. Terms such as 'turn taking', 'turn building', 'turn design' and 'passing the floor from one to the next'. It was the action of 'turn taking' that piqued my interest the most because it is vitally important for the effectiveness of any conversation.

We tend to think that when one person talks, the other listens and then the roles are switched. Interruptions are a problem and expose a lack of active listening, diminishing the quality of the exchange and are just plain rude. However, it's not quite this simple. It is incredibly normal for us to overlap each other's speech ('mm', 'yeah!') to show enthusiasm or just to support the person talking and indicate you are following and understanding what is being said. Sometimes an interruption stops someone continuing temporarily ('Hang on – do you mean this week or next week?'). It's important to distinguish between a stereotypical interruption and a supportive overlap. Since there are typically only milliseconds between turns, it follows that silence between them can speak volumes.

There is a rhythmic to and fro that comes with conversation and turn taking is at the percussive heart of a healthy exchange of words. We constantly and tacitly monitor these turn-taking patterns in order to participate in any conversation. Some may interject rather than interrupt in order to make a small point or ask a question without ruining the other speaker's flow entirely, whereas others will dominate a conversation by not following the tacit turn-taking rules or display their lack of interest in whatever the conversation is about. There are a wide range of social cues and body language (which the Professor tells me are collectively called 'embodied conduct') that we consciously and unconsciously monitor (or deliberately ignore, to hog the floor!) to ensure that when we talk and listen to each other we join the flow of social interaction with the least friction and smoothest progress, like cars joining a motorway.

Professor Stokoe explained that it is often a challenge

to get people to stop and think about what they're saying because, as she said, 'We all talk and we've all got plenty of views about communication already.' As the act of talking comes naturally to the majority of us, we see no need to dive deeper into its mechanisms and therefore may carry on making the same mistakes. So I asked how do we then simply and effectively point out the differences between a 'good' and a 'bad' conversation and illustrate what a good one should look like?

She immediately corrected my use of these two emotive, judgemental and decidedly unacademic words. She advised me to use the more scientifically robust terms, such as what is 'effective' and 'less effective', and gave me her latest favourite analogy to describe what an effective conversation should look like:

Visualise a dog, its owner, a field and a hot-air balloon. Imagine that you are sat in the basket hanging from beneath the hot-air balloon floating above the field which is regularly used by dog walkers. Because this is a fairly well-trodden route, you can see the path that has been made through the field and can surmise the point at which both dog and owner enter the field and where they both leave the field in the most direct and linear way. You cannot, of course, predict the dog's behaviour from your vantage point just below the clouds, but you can see where they will both eventually end up. You now look down and see that a dog owner has one of those long retractable leads and the dog isn't playing ball in terms of discipline; it is running all over the field chasing a ball and the poor owner is having to follow this pesky pooch's zigzags which are constantly veering from the path. Even though you know that they will both eventually end up leaving the field at the opposite end to where they entered, it is rather chaotic to witness. Now picture the same dog and dog owner moving frictionlessly across the field in an effortless route from one point to another. You can immediately conceptualise which one of those two storylines typifies the kind of conversations we should aspire to be having.

'So, for me,' she explained, 'an effective conversation is one that generates the least misunderstanding, the least friction, the least need to do the thing again. And the least tension and friction and misunderstandings as you make progress together across the arc of interaction.' Two people in an effective conversation are the dog and the owner moving in unison across that field. I'll leave it up to you to decide who is the dog and who is the owner in your next social interaction.

We often think that to discuss the important things and experience uplifting moments of connection, we need to first be able to build a meaningful human connection with our interlocutor, otherwise our verbal interplay will lack depth and/or feel unsatisfactory. But the Professor believes this is a common misconception: 'Rapport is the outcome of a really good conversation, not the basis of it.' And the data proves it: 'The best encounters are ones where both parties make fitted responses to everything that the other one does.'

To illustrate her point, she gives the example of walking into a café and ordering a tea. In the first café, having ordered her tea and sat down, she realises that she wants to use the Wi-Fi. She approaches the counter and asks the person serving if they have Wi-Fi. Their response is a simple 'yes', with no further information given, which then prompts a further question of whether customers can use the Wi-Fi. This bored barista, who is presumably having a bad day, just points to the Wi-Fi code on the wall. Not a great experience. But then in another cafe, as they hand over the tea, the person working there says without prompting, 'If you need the Wi-Fi, here's the code.' This is a very short interaction indeed, but it's an important one because it exemplifies the point that Professor Stokoe is trying to make. Even the most basic, brief exchanges can generate warm feelings. The first café worker made Professor Stokoe feel like a burden for having to ask three questions to get to the same result; in the second café, the thoughtfulness, experience and skill of the person pre-empting her question made her feel comfortable and cared about.

What this shows is that a verbal exchange that is devoid of any other social pleasantries, such as 'what's your name?' or 'how are you today?' needn't be one lacking in 'rapport'. Not all conversations require multiple turns that build towards some crescendo of meaning. More, it comes down to the anticipation of what is needed to make that interplay as smooth and direct as possible – not an emotionless exchange, but one that requires the least amount of unnecessary effort. Fitting one action to the previous and next is vital.

Returning to the verbal pugilism that took place between a now former breakfast TV leviathan and a now former government frontbencher, the questioner not only posed the questions but even instructed the listener how to answer them. The health secretary was told that these were questions that simply required a 'yes' or 'no' answer, though the interviewer knew full well that the floundering politician was not going to provide such a response. While the words were all hanging from the same coat hanger, each party attempted to exploit the constraints of the design to meet their own goals for the interview.

Alongside the mistaken belief that building rapport first is essential if effective conversations are to take place, there is a belief, particularly in the corporate sphere, that being 'conversational' means being more informal in the tone and language used. When working with an online questionnaire business, Professor Stokoe was asked about how to make their forms more 'conversational'. She explained that this doesn't mean adding a multitude of exclamation marks and emojis to the questions. 'Instead, I tried to get them to focus on the coat hanger. Conversations emanate from the turn-taking machinery, which is robust and universal. Even a police interrogation is "conversational" from my point of view because it still all has to happen, turn by turn, in an actual conversation.'

I asked her if we can teach ourselves to be better at having conversations, aware that if her response was an immediate 'No, we cannot,' then the entire premise of my book would immediately collapse around me! I drew a sharp intake of breath in anticipation, as Professor Stokoe proceeded to provide me with a specific example of what can go wrong in a conversation and how these mistakes can be pointed out and rectified in future interactions. This concerns a prospective customer calling up to inquire about double glazing. As soon as the salesperson answers the phone, their first question in the dialogue is 'How did you hear about us?' Professor Stokoe told me that the question is in entirely the wrong place in the exchange. It throws the customer because they haven't even been asked by the salesperson what they want and they are immediately having to answer a question which is basically about how effective the company's marketing and advertising strategy is. The conversation then has to be reset before it's begun. Professor Stokoe compared this to the dog dashing around the field and the owner having to chase after it and bring it back onto the path. If the marketing inquiry had been placed at the end of the exchange and couched differently ('Before you go, might you be able to say where you heard about us?'), the chance of the caller feeling like they've built rapport with the salesperson would be much higher, rather than the entitlement of the salesperson almost derailing it from the start. What this tells me is that in any type of social interaction, what gets the participants to communicate most effectively is thinking about what everyone in the conversation needs in order for it to flow with the minimum of friction.

So, that's a very businesslike dialogue, but what about personal conversations between people who know each other well – can we teach ourselves to be better at those? Professor Stokoe took me back to the basics of 'turn taking' and remarked that, 'When it comes to personal life, I think the hardest thing to do is to remember that every single time you take a turn, you do have a choice.' To illustrate the point, she described a scene whereby a man calls his girlfriend and, upon answering the phone, she says in an accusatory tone, 'Hello, where have *you* been all morning?' This is where the concept of choice kicks in. The man has a number of options at his disposal. He could reply defensively, 'What do you mean, where have I been all morning?' Which may light the fuse that leads to an argument exploding. Or he could begin to grovel and apologise for being uncontactable for the previous few hours to try to defuse the situation. He does neither and just says 'Hello!' which brings the forward momentum of her loaded inquiry to an instant stop, although only temporarily. 'But he has a choice,' Professor Stokoe went on to say, 'and that's the really hard thing for us all to remember: that we don't have to join in any conversation in the terms set up by the previous person.'

Essentially, what this means is that once the baton is handed over to you, there is no unwritten rule that dictates your response should run in a direction of their calling. She does admit, though, that making the decision to not be led by the person who speaks before you can be 'really, really hard'. This is because of the control and self-discipline often needed in a situation like this – for example, if the previous speaker was themselves rude, sometimes resisting the temptation to be rude back or calmly calling it out is important. Or perhaps it feels like you are being rude in not being led by the previous speaker, by simply changing direction, with no reference to what has been said before. But deflecting a difficult question, as the example above describes, may defuse anger by not reacting negatively and thus inflaming an already fraught situation, which ultimately protects both speakers from a descent into acrimony and an ineffective conversation.

It is possible to rescue a conversation that is rapidly heading south, as parents have to do all the time, especially when young children are on the verge of a public meltdown in a supermarket aisle or a hormonal teenager is threatening to draw everyone in the immediate vicinity into a huge shouting match. It's worth remembering that we do have a choice – we do not have to be led into a cauldron of boiling-hot words. Acknowledge that you have a choice in how you respond. Although, after a long day at work, returning home hungry and tired to be confronted with a war zone of vitriolic outbursts, I totally understand how you may fail at being the peace negotiator.

Speaking with Professor Stokoe made me think about the structure of a conversation in a way I had never done before. This idea of separating the universal structure of the coat hanger, which forms the basis of all conversations, from the different garments we choose to hang from it made complete sense to me. It was important to see what the rules were that made any conversation an effective one before getting bogged down in the symbolism of every word spoken. The coat hanger was a useful image to think of as a structure which enabled so many different clothes to be hung from it while its shape stayed constant. Please apply this universal structure to how you speak and listen to others and I hope Professor Stokoe's words have given you a greater insight into the mechanics of personal verbal interaction.

After speaking with Professor Stokoe, I reflected on the actual purpose of talking to each other and how the goal is for it to be as frictionless as possible. What we are all attempting to do, after all, is be better communicators. That doesn't mean that when we sit down to talk, everything we say should be bathed in light and positivity. When we know the dialogue will be challenging, it is crucial that we find the most direct route to saying what needs to be said. Professor Stokoe crystallised perfectly the objective of any conversation – at the end of it, the exchange should have been rewarding. By comparing a conversation between two people to a dog and his owner walking side by side across a field as seen from above, she consolidated what it means to have better dialogue into such a simple image. The more confused the conversation, the trickier the dog walk and the less it follows a clear path. The aim is to be mindful of this process and approach each conversation with the knowledge that there are technical ways and means of helping it continue unimpeded in one clear direction. It needn't be down to chance or derailed by saying the wrong words at the wrong time.

We are not automatons, though; we are bound to still get it wrong sometimes. These observations from an expert in her field are not designed to make us feel we are continually falling short of conversational excellence. In fact, from the Professor's point of view, what we might mean by 'conversational excellence' is mostly just stereotypes. Her job involves identifying what people are already doing that is really effective – even if they don't know it at the time. It is inevitable that words will sometimes spill out in the heat of the moment and then we get trapped in the turn-taking sequence. Then the challenge becomes how we use the mechanics of the clothes hanger to change the clothes we choose to place upon it. These skills can be practised and developed. Understanding how conversation actually works 'in the wild' can help us be more aware of the significant benefits to be had for us all by creating increased instances of trust, empathy, love and understanding in our lives. For our mental and physical health, it is critical that we do.

PART 3

CONVERSATIONS IN EXTREMIS

6

Let's Talk About Difficult Conversations

There is a story I always tell that my wife has now heard a million times, though she has perfected the art of pretending to be interested when I recount it in front of strangers. It is a story that illustrates the power of openness and curiosity in building those moments of connection between humans. It is also an anecdote that, due to its reliance on overplaying a sense of danger, makes me feel like a watered-down version of documentary danger-magnet Ross Kemp every time I recite it.

In 2013, when I was still a BBC Radio 1 DJ, the station asked me to host a discussion in Derry/Londonderry (as it always had to be referred to in order to keep both sides and neither side of the sectarian divide happy) with a room full of really inspiring young people from Northern Ireland. This non-music event was taking place as a part of the BBC's commitment to discovering what young people in that region of the UK thought of a number of issues. The hotel we were staying at seemed to lie on the fault line that separated the Catholic and Protestant parts of the city. If you exited one way you would be in the predominantly Protestant area known as the Fountain estate, but if your instincts took you in another direction you were in the Bogside, a sprawling, working-class Catholic estate sitting outside the city walls.

As you enter this part of Northern Island, there are instant reminders of 'the Troubles' that have plagued the region for decades. The memories are seared into the consciousness of its inhabitants and writ large on the walls. Any visitor is immediately presented with giant murals featuring portraits of men and women caught up in the violence of Bloody Sunday and one giant, monochrome message covering the entire side of a house that simply reads 'You Are Now Entering Free Derry' – the mural being a self-declared statement of independence from the British, dating back to the 1970s.

We had been told not to leave the hotel without informing a member of the BBC team, which would have almost certainly led to me being told not to leave the hotel and absolutely not to stray into the Bogside, so, partly due to what could be described as naïve optimism, I ignored that and went off to wander around an area I had heard so much about. My quick-fire risk analysis told me that a Catholic area would be safer for me than a Protestant one, due to historic Protestant paramilitary links to the far right. It was an assessment; I never said it was a sophisticated one. So I ventured into the Bogside alone and wide-eyed. Having grown up in a village in Essex, I was used to being stared at, so the cars that slowed down to gawp didn't bother me, as who wouldn't think 'What the bloody hell is an Asian fella doing walking alone through the Bogside on a Sunday afternoon?!'

As I meandered through this infamous and deeply symbolic part of Northern Ireland, I couldn't help but notice a particularly uninviting building called The Bogside Inn. As I walked past it, the risk-versus-reward calculations began to appear in my brain. The risk being that I could get a really good hiding for having the temerity to encroach upon the hallowed ground of the local community's most intimate drinking establishment; the reward being I could use this anecdote for a book. Reward triumphed over risk and I strode towards the door with purpose in my eyes and knots in my stomach.

In the seconds before reaching the precipice of the door, my overactive imagination went into overdrive and pictured the scene quite clearly. The dark stranger enters, the Celtic flute player (silly stereotype) stops instantly, the dusty old regulars' necks snap in unison as they collectively focus their gaze on this mysterious interloper. After the landlord exclaims, 'You ain't from round these parts, are ya?!' a brief but focused fracas occurs, and the alien presence is subsequently and unceremoniously ejected via an unopened window, crashing onto the hard tarmac floor of the street outside. The one thing I had going for me as I neared the entrance was that, as far as I can recollect, The

Bogside Inn appeared to be windowless, so at least I knew I'd be ejected via the door.

As I approached, I noticed a man stood outside smoking. He looked like a character from one of those documentaries with titles such as 'Britain's Scariest Men'. I sheepishly asked this imposing-looking man if it would be OK if I entered. He looked me up and down and then replied, 'Why wouldn't it be?' in a tone that managed to combine being unwelcoming, menacing and begrudgingly hospitable simultaneously.

As predicted, everybody inside did indeed stop and stare. I immediately felt conscious of how different I looked to everyone else in there. There was no Celtic flute player. After a few minutes of being ignored by the bartender, one of the regulars, a very friendly older lady who had noticed that I was patiently waiting, called over to the woman on the staff side of the bar and asked me what I wanted to drink. I wish that I had ordered a whisky as alcohol would have probably steadied my nerves, but I ordered an orange juice because I was working that evening and I get drunk very easily.

A few more minutes passed and a man who clearly couldn't control his curiosity any longer walked up to me and asked the question I am sure everybody in The Bogside Inn that afternoon wanted answering. 'Where are you from?' Dressed in a black Belstaff Fieldmaster jacket with the collar up, I looked as out of place as an undercover drugs officer at a techno rave. I had to quickly find a response that would satiate his need for information and hopefully not prompt further inquiry. 'I live in London' was the best answer I had, which clearly satisfied nobody's curiosity as it was hardly a revelation that I wasn't a local. Straight off the bat, he responded with the classic secondary question, one that people of colour are used to being asked, usually implying a more unsettling sentiment: that we are actually a foreigner and have confused residence with heritage. In this instance, though, I felt that he was justified in seeking further clarification of my origins. He had already dismissed my first answer as irrelevant and then said quite robustly, 'No, where are you really from?!' This follow-up question is, of course, always melanin-related, so I always respond with the honest answer, which is, 'My parents are from Sri Lanka.' On hearing the words 'Sri' and 'Lanka', his face lit up and at the top of his voice he perfectly pronounced out loud the name 'Sangakkara!' albeit with a broad Northern Irish accent.

For the uninitiated, Kumar Sangakkara is one of the greatest cricketers to have ever played the game, a former captain of Sri Lanka, president of the Marylebone Cricket Club and a national hero to all the Sri Lankans I know. So there I was, in The Bogside Inn, in the Bogside, in Derry, in Northern Ireland and I had managed to find not only a cricket fan, in a country not known for its love of the game, but one who revered one of Sri Lanka's greatest ever humans.

As the word 'Sangakkara!' warmly and triumphantly reverberated from every wall of the pub, there was a collective sigh of relief from all in attendance. It instantly felt like every eye that had been focused on me drifted back to whatever it had been looking at before my arrival and the atmosphere changed from one of cautious inquisitiveness to acceptance. We stood and chatted about sport in general, I drank up, bid my farewells and genuinely felt pretty damn happy with myself as I walked back to the hotel. I distinctly remember the receptionist asking me if I had been on a nice walk and as I said the words 'Bogside' and 'Inn', he was visibly taken aback and said, 'Even I wouldn't go in there.'

While not being on the scale of embedding myself with Colombian drug lords or far-right Russian football hooligans, this moment has always stood with me as an example of having to sometimes put yourself in what you perceive to be a potentially challenging space in order to derive a connection with someone who you would have previously felt you could have nothing in common with. While my actual conversation in The Bogside Inn that Sunday afternoon was neither profound nor long-lasting, it had a profound and long-lasting effect on me.

So often we prevent ourselves from entering into physical spaces because our experiences, prejudices and insecurities get the better of us. Moving from one racially segregated area into another where the majority does not resemble you. Wandering into the rougher parts of town that you've been warned against entering. Or, on the flip side, finding yourself on a high street in an affluent area lined with stylish boutiques that you find too intimidating to enter. Whether they be cultural, ethnic or financial differences, the end result is the same: you feel uncomfortable. The tendency we humans have to huddle into groups that we feel comfortable with is both understandable and in some aspects essential. But I cannot overstate how much it has enriched my life to have placed myself in situations interacting with people who have lived a completely different life to my own. An afternoon spent in a Shia Muslim school for children with special needs in southern Lebanon. Talking to the long white-haired owner of a dusty old art gallery in Zimbabwe. Or walking through the muddy, litter-strewn alleys of Africa's biggest slum on a Sunday morning, watching families in their cleanest, smartest clothes make their way to church.

The fear of entering certain places isn't just confined to a pub, an estate, a city or an entire country. The most valuable conversations themselves are spaces where the participants give over a part of themselves to each other to explore, illuminate and connect. As a man of Sri Lankan heritage born and bred in England, I thought that I would have little in common with the denizens of a pub in a socially, religiously and politically segregated part of Northern Ireland. That experience, even though it lasted less than an hour, has stuck with me ever since. A brown man walks into a white area. A Buddhist in a Catholic stronghold. An Essex boy in Derry. A set of middle-class experiences in a resolutely working-class environment. A community that has seen such hardship, felt so much pain and endured more turmoil than any group of people should have to go through. And yet my openness to new experiences and their curiosity certainly reinforced my belief that being curious and open cannot help but enrich your life.

Of course, the sectarian divide still exists in Northern Ireland, but we should never forget that every day there are people who are trying to build bridges of trust and respect. These people refuse to allow hatred and communalism to become so hardwired into the fabric of society that it would be a useless endeavour to even attempt a rapprochement of any kind. Cast your mind back to the nineties in Northern Ireland, if you can, and the months and years that preceded the signing of the Good Friday Agreement on 10 April 1998, which effectively brought an end to the three-decade-long era of violence known as 'the Troubles'. Think about how difficult it must have been for those individuals who believed in peace to look into the eyes of the people who had once wanted them dead. Imagine the courage it takes to try to compartmentalise your feelings towards a person who had, on possibly more than one occasion, tried to put that hatred into practice with bullets and bombs.

I'm probably not making too wild an assumption that you have not had to sit across the table from people who would once have tried to kill you and your family. Would I be right in thinking that you have not had to reach out to and then find yourself with a group of people who hate you for your gender, ethnicity and/or faith? Do you believe that you have it in you to become someone who would be willing to try to uncover the person beneath the bigotry?

What about trying to create the right environment for a high-stakes conversation with a person who is intent on taking the lives of others, or taking their own, knowing that a failure on your part to connect could well result in disaster?

In this chapter, we turn our attention to people who have had some of the most difficult conversations imaginable. Dialogues that lives depend on, words uttered that can change the course of history. Sometimes undertaken by people who wished to look hate directly in the eyes and try to comprehend where that hatred came from. In hearing from these people, what can we understand about our own difficult relationships, where trust has broken down and only enmity remains? An insult at a family gathering that stubbornly refuses to disappear over time, a relationship with someone not approved of by your family, a prejudiced relative whose views are diametrically opposed to your own.

There is a myriad of reasons to explain why human connection breaks down, gulfs appear and time simply exacerbates rather than heals the rifts. By focusing on some extreme examples, I want to try to understand how, in even the most unlikely of circumstances, a connection can be made by simply talking to each other – but also how important it is to be methodical when selecting the words you use. The self-control required to listen intently before responding. To unpick the meaning without trying to predict the response and then mistakenly preparing the answer ahead of time. To live in the moment while being aware of the future repercussions. To overcome the instinct to lobby and cajole. Such endeavours are not without heartache, rancour and cynicism, but I hope that by the end of this chapter you will think about the difficult conversations that you are yet to have and find some solace, or even a route towards a better relationship with someone you have fallen out with.

7

Mary McAleese:
Drawing Paramilitaries into the Peace Process

In October 2020, the former president of Ireland Mary McAleese was a guest on my BBC radio show to discuss her memoir *Here's the Story* and we had a wide-ranging and powerful conversation about her life. It was an interview that stayed with me to such an extent that I immediately thought of reaching out to her when it came to writing this chapter on the most difficult of conversations. Her story was an all-too-familiar example of the hurdles that people have to overcome in order to move on from a past that will destroy their future if not challenged.

Imagine that the streets that you grew up around and wandered out to play in changed before your very eyes. In a relatively short space of time, rather than simply being the tarmac arteries that people and vehicles flowed along, these very streets became 'bloodstained battlegrounds', as she describes the Ardoyne area of North Belfast, where she was born and raised, in her memoir. To leave no doubt in your mind as to the extent of the violence that the teen-age, and then young adult, Mary McAleese witnessed, in the early seventies, this predominantly Catholic working-class community 'became the area with the highest per capita incidence of sectarian murders'. According to num-bers cited in Mary's book, in 1969 there were eighteen violent deaths across Northern Ireland. The following twelve months saw twenty-eight people killed, twenty of those by Republican paramilitaries. By 1971, 180 people had lost their lives through sectarian violence. In 1972, across Northern Ireland, 496 people were killed, half of those civilians. Between 1969 and 1998, when the Good Friday Agreement was signed and the Northern Ireland Assembly was set up, 3,720 had been killed as a result of the conflict. During that almost thirty-year period, over 16,000 bombings and nearly 37,000 shootings took place, and tens of thousands of people were injured. This was the backdrop to Mary's and so many of her compatriots' lives. For her, it was not a fleeting story on a TV news bulletin or a fictionalised account on a cinema screen: 'the Troubles' were in her neighbourhood, on her street and even in the supposed safety of her family home.

Generation upon generation learned to mistrust their fellow citizens. Both physical and psychological walls were built to segregate people from one another based on religion and divergent ideologies and histories. These details are important because the brutal events that took place bring into sharp focus just how monumental the task must have been, and still continues to be, to build trust and foster reconciliation. This was an environment which could breed hate and mistrust on an industrial scale, as neighbours became enemies and communities withdrew themselves from one another.

More than five decades after a teenage Mary McAleese witnessed the descent of her neighbourhood and her country into a maelstrom of violence, we sat down and faced each other through computer screens to have a conversation about difficult conversations. She was so gracious in giving up her time to speak to me about a subject she had not only written a book about but spent much of her adult life talking about. Speaking not just about herself but describing how indoctrinated everyone was, Mary began by saying: 'From very early on, we were the recruits into one version of history, into one version of politics, into one version of religion.' With such a deeply engrained partisan identity, where do you even begin to build a dialogue with people who had been dehumanised to the point of seeing you purely as an enemy, and vice versa? How could you reach out to the most hard-headed of your foes, the ones who would broach no compromise, now sitting around the same table as you?

Her answer was a pragmatic one, immediately relieving me of the notion that you could start with those people. You do not begin with the extremists. The gulf in trust was so wide and the enmity so deep that no amount of goodwill would bring them to you initially. No, the key was to find those who were willing to listen and build a bridge with them. They would not be easily identifiable or instantly onside, but at least their minds would be partially open to the concept of having a conversation. As Mary told me, her job, and that of many others, was to set out their stall from the beginning and allay the understandable fears of those they wanted to speak with: 'We wanted to build up credibility that we were about the business of building good neighbourliness only and not about proselytising or trying to change anybody's politics.' Mary and her colleagues had to get to a stage whereby the people deemed potentially receptive to breaching the divide could arrive at a place of mutuality. These Protestant groups would still be cautious and potentially wary of her motives but not so much so that no conversation could take place.

Perhaps unsurprisingly, vital common ground between the two communities lay just under the surface, as the mutual antagonism of the past gave way to a shared view of what the future could and should look like – 'And that was the big discovery.' It all began with a question: 'When you focus on the future, what kind of world do you want for your children?' The answer was as simple as it was revelatory: 'We all wanted our children to be able to walk the streets with freedom not to feel threatened.' As she spoke the words out loud, it seemed so obvious that this sentiment would cut through. Those who sat across the table had, like Mary, grown up knowing violence, fear and suspicion. Whether Catholic or Protestant, they had an unenviable shared experience of what it felt like to see a loved one leave home and not know if they would return that evening. As far too many never did. Having felt that degree of dread-induced suffocation, why would anyone wish for their children to inherit the same levels of anxiety and trauma?

Those preliminary exchanges had to be more fundamental and constructive than a simple list of grievances that required the other to offer some sort of penance in exchange for the granting of favours. And there could be no obvious hierarchical element. To insist upon a reverence for political titles and educational qualifications would have been counterproductive. 'We weren't negotiating in the sense of trying to bring about a political reconciliation,' explained Mary, 'we were trying to bring about a human reconciliation.' It was clearly understood by all that the process was never going to be an easy or straightforward one. Impetuousness and impatience would have to be parked at the door, and decades of animosity would not be overcome through a few nice words and select photo opportunities. It was a process that evolved over many years as, level by level, the invitees went from, as Mary describes it: 'The people who were willing to come, then the less willing, then the very unwilling, bit by bit by bit, building up confidence and credibility.' Through this gradual process of seeking to build a base camp with one set of individuals before attempting the next stage of the climb, eventually the time was right to connect with the most difficult group of people to bring onside: the paramilitaries themselves.

In sensitive situations such as these, there must be an ever-present risk of self-sabotaging the proceedings by allowing inherited discontent and the placing of unrealistic expectations on both parties to derail the entire process. If such feelings are given space to fester and then burst into the open, the inevitable breakdown occurs and the road back to a place of agreement gets that little bit longer and harder to navigate. In the face of what was already a complex process, the office of the President of Ireland and the representatives of the Protestant community in Northern Ireland understood that simplicity and a managing of expectations was the key: 'Our view was just do what's doable, figure out how you're going to get in touch with those people, how you're going to draw them into conversation and hold them in conversation, and how you are going to create a relationship with them that ultimately is based on trust.'

Methodical, orchestrated, open-minded and welcoming was the intention, but this must have been more easily said than done. Such ventures are hard-fought, even though on the surface they may seem to follow an orthodox route to completion. I asked Mary what she thought the artistry of getting the two sides together was. At the heart of her answer was the simple truth of what will help you evolve into being a great conversationalist. It is what I believe to be the single most important skill that you will need in order to truly benefit conversationally from the myriad of relationships that surround you. She said: 'What I think really worked for us was the fact that my husband Martin was willing to go and listen to them. Just to sit and listen. The very fact that he did while they [the paramilitaries] were not on ceasefire was itself quite remarkable.'

It is worth noting that the work that Martin McAleese did in engaging with Loyalist paramilitaries had such a long-lasting effect on them that, in 2011, the then leader of the Ulster Defence Association, Jackie McDonald, a man who Martin had visited, spoken to and played golf with alongside other paramilitaries in order to build trust, actually said on record that Martin would be the 'perfect candidate' to take over from Mary McAleese as president of Ireland. Martin's actions demonstrated his belief in the cause but also great bravery, as he travelled to the very men who had at that point expressed no wish to renounce violence. This was human connection that required so much more than passive engagement.

What do we miss out on when we do not listen, when the social media algorithm projects our unchallenged thoughts onto the screen? Far too many people have become accustomed to launching their views out into the world as if every opinion that leaves their mind has unimpeachable validity. In polite company, the people surrounding the opinion transmitter may just courteously absorb the verbal outpourings this person feels all around must benefit from hearing, as they do not wish to appear rude, but when the people being addressed mistrust the other person's motives for being there and could even be hostile to the speaker, as was found through the peace process, then the impetus should be to listen more than talk. In the process of seeking commonality, the desire to be right has to be replaced by the need to be open and to be willing to jettison some of your own preconceived thoughts.

When Mary speaks, it is with the calm authority of the lawyer, but contained within that is always a zeal that exposes the purposefulness of every action. The former president of Ireland couldn't have been clearer with the message she wanted to get across: 'I'm coming to you not as somebody who wants to change who you are, what you are and what you believe in; I want to come as a good neighbour to accept you, and by you inviting me, you also accept me on my terms.'

In the case of negotiations of this magnitude, the questions around where such gatherings could take place also had to be taken into account. The conversations were important, but buildings have histories and symbolism attached, and the past associations of bricks and mortar couldn't be allowed to disrupt the possibilities for the future. The men and women willing to talk to the eighth president of Ireland would not leave their Protestant enclaves north of the border to be lectured to in the hallowed halls of municipal buildings in Dublin. It would be unthinkable for representatives of the Unionist community to sit under the elaborate ceilings of Leinster House – home to both houses of the Irish Parliament: the Dáil and the Senate. As has already been said, that would frame the entire conversation as a political rather than human one. Simplicity again was the key: 'We decided from the beginning that we would invite people to our home. We would sit around, have a cup of tea and we wouldn't talk about the hard stuff; we would talk about children, holidays, the weather. We would talk about anything but the hard stuff initially.'

That may work for community leaders, but what about the reputational risks inherent in inviting paramilitaries into your home? An elected representative of the people could not be seen to be engaging with men of violence in such an openly hospitable way. From the start, Mary McAleese understood that these men could not be treated any differently to those who had not been engaged in violence. The greater risk was failing to secure a lasting peace and that trumped any superficial risks associated with public perception. 'For those who were paramilitaries, we would bring them through the front door. There was no question of bringing them through side doors or trapdoors or back doors,' she recounted.

I have already asked you to imagine the bravery required to enter into this process; now think about what it takes to invite people through your front door who just years before would've shot their way through that door or attempted to blow up that house in its entirety, and yet here they were invited in as equals. We should also recognise how difficult it must have been for the paramilitaries that were willing to talk, knowing that there were members of their community who were still hell-bent on achieving their political goals through violence.

On both sides, there had to be a gradual casting-off of past prejudices in order to begin the steps of leaving that old life behind and creating an entirely new one. Of course, not everybody who came through the front door bought into the idea of needing compromise to find a solution. But everyone who did was asked to come back next time and bring ten of their friends with them. In that way, ripples of positivity spread out across the community, scepticism subsided and progress was made.

Interestingly, in addition to those initial conversations across the sectarian divide, social occasions and outings were organised, such as a tour of a Japanese garden, attending a football match, watching a horse race. These proved so much more powerful than PowerPoint presentations, data analysis and pre-agreed agendas. Just think of the times that you have found yourself in a conversation with a stranger and bonded over your shared love of a football team, a musician or even a particularly niche corner of the horticultural world. (Or a Sri Lankan cricketer.) These very human connections form a basic foundation of trust – not a guarantee of it, certainly, but a positive place to start. I am not a relationship expert, as my wife would certainly attest, but if there is a breakdown between two people, then taking it back to the areas of our lives where, away from religion, skin colour or politics, we can find a bond that helps us to recognise our similarities can only be a good thing. The two sides of the conflict in Northern Ireland had been shaped by very real, deep-rooted and damaging experiences, and these had previously prevented the possibility of those points of togetherness happening. What Mary and many like her were attempting to do was to reconnect through the elements of their lives that they could share – a cup of tea, a trip to a garden, a dream of a less damaged and violent country to bequeath to their children. 'Little by little, we hoped that in doing those very human things they would speak well of us in their community. We were hopefully building trust and, out of that trust, we would hopefully be investing in a non-sectarian future where, whether you were Catholic or Protestant unionist or nationalist, you weren't afraid of each other.'

In all of the paramilitarism, machismo and violence, I wonder how many times those on either side would have admitted to being scared of the other. In all of the posturing and very real acts of aggression that took place, would they have been able to say out loud that fear stalked the streets, darkened the neighbourhoods and oppressed the lives of so many people?

My next question to Mary McAleese was a vital one. I asked her how much introspection is needed when approaching a difficult conversation. Before asking what you deem to be the most difficult question of your adversary, what of the really difficult ones that you have to ask of yourself? Presumably there had to be an acceptance of what she needed to change about herself, a move to understanding her own biases and prejudices, and that she would need to overcome these in order to build that bridge. 'I think the process of unlearning, the self-critiquing, the unlearning of all the baggage that you carry yourself, that's just absolutely an important part of it.'

If you believe yourself to be the only victim in the equation, then that immediately closes you off to understanding or accepting the experiences of the person you believe to be your enemy. It was a point that Mary was keen to make in our conversation. 'Many people on both sides of the political equation see themselves as the sole victims and that's the danger. The other imposes victimhood and we absorb victimhood. We had to strip away from ourselves the assumption that what we had endured belongs only to our community.'

I was keen to home in on those first conversations with the paramilitaries themselves. Having moved on from the political representatives, what would happen once the time came to sit in front of someone that would have initially been the one most reluctant to talk peace, the one for whom violence was the only way of achieving their intended goals?

The Good Friday Agreement was, of course, not the end of the story – much work had to be done once the politicians had left Belfast to continue the job of building trust between communities, and the eighth president of Ireland spent almost every day of her 14 years in the job from 1997 to 2011 attempting to achieve the goal of building trust and reconciliation.

A perfect illustration of how far the two parties had already come was in the giving of gifts. When the first group of Loyalist paramilitaries arrived at the house of the president, they brought her a Glasgow Rangers scarf.

Anyone who is *au fait* with the politics of football knows that Rangers are strongly associated with the Protestant community. This small act of ironic gift-giving illustrates the power of in-person conversations to completely change a relationship.

It is important to note that such advances did not erase the structural impediments that existed. According to Mary, barriers of mistrust were created by a lack of formal education on the part of many of the paramilitaries. It became apparent to her and others that these men were nervous around people who had degrees, masters, and doctorates. Then there was also the lack of a defined hierarchical structure to contend with – how could you be certain that you were talking to people who had influence in their communities? Understanding the community, identifying those who had influence and simply reaching out to them seems to have worked.

After inviting these men into her residence, it was inevitable that at some point she would have to reciprocate and travel into their territory. As a native of Northern Ireland, she knew these areas well. If these conversations were to mean anything at all, there had to be a willingness of both parties to cross physical borders, as well as those of the mind. This was not without risk, but that gatherings such as this were even possible was a testament to the depth of the work that had already been put in to break down animosity and suspicion. 'I went to a tough Loyalist estate in Belfast. They got in touch and said we have flags up – Union Jacks and Ulster flags. Do you want us to take them down? And I said no, let me return the compliment of respect.'

Generations of engrained enmity were being dismantled in order to find common ground – but it was also crucial to foster a respect for difference. If the outcome you desire from a conversation is for the person you're speaking with to change to be more like you, then it should be self-evident that the conversation is doomed. People across Northern Ireland had to teach themselves to be better listeners, through hard work, perseverance, introspection and empathy. Throughout the process – which is still ongoing – both sides had to remember the fundamental basics of who they needed to be for the peace process to be a success, not necessarily who they felt compelled to be because of the historical issues that had plagued the region for decades.

As we face the fractious worlds of politics, the culture war and social media, it is important to remember what Mary said about her approach to the process of reconciliation and what she wanted those sitting across from her to understand about her: 'I'm coming to you not as somebody who wants to change you, who you are, what you are, what you believe in, what your politics are or your identifying symbols; I want to come as a good neighbour.'

Nothing better illustrates the power contained within meaningful conversations to completely transform the landscape than former enemies beginning to share a vision.

From a barren wasteland pockmarked with the memories of embittered confrontations, people found hope. These weren't groups who willingly held hands as they skipped towards a perceived utopia. The men and women who wanted a different future for their children were realists, pragmatists and good listeners.

In May 2011, President Mary McAleese sat next to Her Majesty the Queen at a state banquet at Dublin Castle. As it was the first state visit of a British monarch in the history of both countries, it was an evening of some magnitude. Before the Queen stood up to give her speech – the first five words of which were in Ulster Irish, a hugely symbolic moment in itself – President McAleese welcomed the Queen by saying: 'This visit is the culmination of the success of the peace process. It is an acknowledgement that, while we cannot change the past, we have chosen to change the future.'

Peace is fragile, something we all too often forget, but as long as people believe that there can be a better future, then there is scope for the talking to begin. But it takes people with the courage of Mary McAleese, her husband Martin McAleese and a host of others to go through the process of confronting their own prejudices, displaying a genuine openness and understanding the power of simple acts of kindness and generosity. These aren't superpowers possessed by only a few; they are learned behaviours, just as the more negative ones are that pollute communities. Mary McAleese was one of my first choices of people to be interviewed for this book because the part she played in achieving reconciliation against the odds is the clearest demonstration of just how powerful our words are when used wisely.

8

Deeyah Khan:
Sitting Down with Neo-Nazis

In December 2017, the brown-skinned, female, Muslim film-maker Deeyah Khan's extraordinary documentary *White Right: Meeting The Enemy* premiered on British TV. It went on to win an Emmy, was BAFTA-nominated and universally lauded as a brave, deeply personal and journalistically outstanding example of documentary film-making. The reason it is relevant to mention her skin colour, gender and the faith that she was born into is because to make the documentary, she decided to travel to North America and engage with a selection of people who hated her for being all of those things.

Rather than spend her life quite understandably trying to avoid such individuals, Deeyah Khan wanted to sit down with men who would almost certainly despise her on sight. Their feelings towards her were fuelled by their perception of the existence of a clash of civilisations. In the literature they read, the online groups they belonged to and the social circles they mingled in, people like Deeyah were an attack on their way of life and, to some extent, their very existence. Their world view resulted in such a deep-rooted mistrust that they would most likely be unable to see her as a fellow human being, but instead view her as a selection of labels, such as 'invader', 'immigrant' and 'terrorist sympathiser'. And yet she set out to film these meetings, taking place in raw and intimate settings. Without knowing how she would be received, whether she would be treated courteously or even be physically safe, she stuck her head into the lion's mouth, unsure of the outcome.

At first, I was reticent to sit down and watch her film, but I am so glad that I did. It is difficult to describe how watching it made me feel, but for the purposes of this book I will try to. So often, a film about racism leaves you feeling hollow and pessimistic. Why would you want to spend an hour of your life in the company of (mainly) men who any decent person would cross the street to avoid? Films covering this topic can at times feel formulaic as the film-maker will, albeit with good intentions, present the horror of what modern-day fascism looks like. Angry man after angry man looks down the barrel of the camera and spews forth a litany of ill-conceived, poorly articulated diatribes on racial purity, immigrant criminality and white supremacy. You will see some of these men attend a pseudo-militaristic tribal gathering/training camp of like-minded racists in the middle of nowhere, miles away from the urban centres they despise, and at some point in the documentary, a proud member of what they would no doubt regard to be the 'Aryan race' will give a speech to the cheers of his supporters. You may see jerky camera, phone footage of pitched battles between groups of racists, anti-fascists and the police. Such films are a reminder of the present and a warning of what the future may hold if we are not constantly vigilant, looking for the signs, identifying the perpetrators. These films present the broad political and socio-economic currents that feed such views and they present us with an uncomfortable view of where our own petty prejudices could take us, while we are simultaneously repulsed by where these men's prejudices have taken them. My experience of watching many of these films is that they offer more noise than light.

Deeyah Khan's documentary was different. The men she met up with were not shown simply as two-dimensional racist villains direct from central casting – skinheads, hillbilly accents, long unkempt beards and Confederate flags. As a viewer, you found yourself standing just behind Deeyah, staring at these men from over her shoulder as she peered into their lives, deconstructed their motivations and illuminated their childhood and adolescent experiences. At the beginning, I wanted to dislike these men, to caricature them as rednecks who were beyond saving. They were abhorrent individuals who had been emboldened by the belief that the forty-fifth president of the United States was, at the very least, sympathetic to their views. But as the documentary progressed, I found myself wanting to know more about them, how it came to be that they were so angry with the world and what really underpinned their hatred for Muslims, Jews, homosexuals and anyone else who didn't conform to their very narrow opinion of how the world should be.

As Deeyah peeled back layer after layer, it became obvious that the people they hated more than anyone else were themselves. The film-maker wasn't a counsellor, a therapist or a psychologist, she wanted to know them as people and to try to understand how they had become the people who now sat in front of her. It would not be an exaggeration to describe my emotional state by the end of the film as hopeful bordering on euphoric. Never before had I had this experience with a documentary with the subject of racism at its core. It was hopeful, it was humane and it rekindled in me a belief that through discovering a human connection, there is a potential to find a fundamental goodness in people you would have believed were wholly lacking it. However deeply buried that goodness may be under layers of hurt, frustration and anger.

Even though some of these men felt empowered by the new iconoclast in the Oval Office, the impetus to make a film of this kind did not begin with the election of Donald Trump to the White House in 2016. This story has its origins in the childhood of a little brown girl growing up in a predominantly white country. When she was six years old, Deeyah's Pakistani immigrant father took her to an anti-racist rally in his new home country of Norway. Her father, who was presumably an optimist, told his young daughter that the skinhead gangs who were wreaking havoc in immigrant neighbourhoods would one day be a thing of the past and that the future would be one of tolerance. As a grown woman, Deeyah's frustration was that this future that her father had described still hadn't arrived, three decades on from her attending that march with him. In fact, not just in her home country but across the western world, race relations looked to be regressing.

Deeyah grew up all too aware of what the words and actions of the bigots looked and felt like. As an adult and a film-maker, she wanted to look these men (they were almost entirely men) in the eyes and try to see who they were underneath the bravado, the uniforms, the slogans and the tattoos. This wasn't in order to foster a peace process and to bring whole communities together, undertaken as a self-proclaimed representative of a minority group or a martyr for the anti-fascist cause. This was a deeply personal journey to try to understand where the hate came from. To see if there could be any human connection between a brown Muslim woman and a white racist man. As with Mary McAleese, it also needed to begin with a self-examination of her own place in this world. The title of the documentary, *Meeting the Enemy*, didn't just apply to her meeting her enemies, those who hated her very existence; it contained the acceptance that to these people, she too was an enemy, and all the suspicion, fear and mistrust that she harboured towards them was most likely being felt by them towards her.

'I think my job in a way was to try to invite out somehow who they really are past the chest-beating Naziness of it. So who are you really and what is it in you that creates this capacity for you to reside in this sort of space and dehumanise other people to the extent that you do?'

Of course, they were suspicious of her from the outset. She had to admit to herself that there was nothing that she could do, certainly in the short term, to change those feelings of antipathy. As with the former President of Ireland, Deeyah knew that patience and presence was key. Patience was obvious, but the physical reality of her being in their space created a different dynamic. They had to be in close proximity to each other – one with a camera, the other looking at her through their own lens of fear, judgement and mistrust. Deeyah's subjects had in their minds exactly how they would be portrayed, as there were countless examples of how such documentaries had presented them in the past. Deeyah explained what those initial meetings were like and said something that I found intriguing: 'Their humanity is always removed from how they are presented. They thought I was going to dehumanise them and judge them and condemn them out of the gate.'

This is what made her documentary so life-affirming, and so fascinating. From the very start, Deeyah knew that a shared space, a genuine one, was what was needed. She knew that there would be no magic words that could instantly dilute all of that pent-up animosity but thought that physical proximity may help: 'Once we come into contact with each other, spend some more meaningful time together, actually really engage with each other, does something else become possible or not? Can they see my humanity and can I see theirs?' Deeyah knew what needed to be done and was exhilarated by the prospect of what such an investment of time and energy could deliver.

At this point, I could cloak myself in a gilded gown of self-righteousness as I extol the virtues of always searching for the humanity in those who would try to belittle me, call me a 'diversity hire' or downright deny the fact I belong in the UK at all. But anyone who has followed me on social media over the last decade knows that I don't react well to that kind of bigotry. When I am racially attacked on Twitter, I tend to come out fighting. Rather than defuse the situation, my default has always been reminiscent of the playground fights in which I used to proclaim very loudly that if you thought that I was going to be a doormat for you to wipe your shoes on, then, to use a more contemporary phrase, 'I ain't the one, son!' When a fellow pupil called me a 'Paki', more often than not the fists would start flying. Similarly, every time an internet troll would goad me, I would be straight back there in the corridors of an Essex comprehensive school, or on the school bus, or in the playground, defending myself in the only way that made sense to me.

The problem is that social media isn't just one person that you can have a fight with and then make up with. It becomes a swarm of parasites all feeding on negativity and division. I am also now an adult. In the short term, violence can sometimes seem to be the easier route out of the problem, despite what some people might say. At school it worked on a few occasions. A good friend of mine, who is a former member of the elite Parachute Regiment of the British Army, once told me, 'Never write cheques with your mouth that your fists can't cash.' More than once, I enjoyed writing out those cheques more than I liked cashing them. The longer and more difficult journey is to stick in there with grace and dignity when your antagonist wants a more confrontational reaction from you. At school, this is defined as a form of cowardice by your would-be persecutors. As an adult, it becomes vital, however frustrating that may be. Though it takes great reserves of self-control from me, that in the past I have found it very difficult to find.

When Deeyah began filming, she knew that they would try to provoke her: 'They tried to be obnoxious, they tried to push my buttons. They tried to throw me off balance because they wanted to get the reactions that they are used to getting.' The men who stood before her wanted the conversations to be about the politics, the anger, the resentment. It was a chance to expound their manifesto, to project and perform. They wanted to verbally control and dominate the dialogue, to keep it in a space that they were familiar with and used to defending. After all, that is all anyone ever really wanted from them, either as an ally or as an enemy. State your position, lean into it and defend it to the last. It would have been so easy to fall into their trap. Voices would be raised and the ensuing cacophony would drown out any hope of a reasonable exchange of ideas or a discovery of commonality. This would be the ideal atmosphere for misinformation and malevolence to thrive.

'And so what did I do?' said Deeyah. 'I would ask them a lot about their earlier life and their family life and their childhood and their experiences in school just to bring the conversation somewhere else and bring it to them.' I asked her what this approach showed those neo-Nazis and white supremacists. 'That I wasn't there to score points,' she replied. 'That I wasn't there to win a match. And maybe it actually was of interest to me what they thought, but more importantly why they thought that, and that's something that they weren't used to.' The first barrier was to get them to talk to her; the second was for them to overcome their mistrust of her; and the third was for them to allow that fear to dissipate by listening to what a female Muslim film-maker actually had to say.

There was one conversation that particularly stood out to Deeyah, with a man called Jeff Schoep, who, at the time of them speaking, was the leader of an American group called the National Socialist Movement – an organisation whose website stated, 'We demand that all non-whites currently residing in America be required to leave the nation forthwith and return to their land of origin: peacefully or by force.' Even before he got to high school, Jeff claimed to have read Hitler's *Mein Kampf*. At nineteen, he joined the snappily titled National Socialist American Workers' Freedom Movement. In 1994, he took over the organisation and rebranded it as the National Socialist Movement. By this stage, he was only twenty-one years old. He was a virulent antisemite but didn't reserve all of his hatred for the Jewish community. For example, he once described the Latino communities in America as 'breeding us out of existence'. So, in summary, a thoroughly unpleasant man.

How could you find common ground with a person like this? Under what circumstances could an individual whose hate for minorities was so deeply engrained change his mind? Where would you even start? Deeyah had to begin by acknowledging that the hurt that he felt was real to him and to those who aligned themselves with his beliefs. Not to agree with his world view but to accept that his grievances were legitimate to him. Jeff spoke at length about how people were really struggling as factories closed down and rampant poverty spread, and that these elements were conspiring to effectively end the American dream for white people. The dream being one that his parents had believed in: that each generation would do better than the previous one. Sitting before Deeyah was a man who genuinely felt that he belonged to the first generation in American history that would in fact be worse off than his parents' one had been. It was then time, of course, to turn his ire towards those who were prospering while he witnessed the demise of his own community. In his mind, these were the immigrants and Black people who benefited from government programmes and affirmative action.

Calmly, without hyperbole or a list of activist sound bites, Deeyah asked him to think of those immigrants and Black people being in exactly the same boat as him. 'You're fighting the same struggle,' she told Jeff. 'You want the same thing. You want to do good for your kids. You want to survive. You want a dignified life. Do you see that?'

It was compassionately pointed out to him that the only thing he shared with the billionaire who occupied the White House then was skin colour. As Deeyah described the parallels between working-class people of all backgrounds – the shared struggle and an economic system that had rendered many of their lives worse than those of the previous generation – it was clear that Jeff didn't have his responses ready to go. You would think that a man so wedded to his cause must surely have been able to bat away the notion that the experiences of his community were in any way comparable to those of immigrant communities, who in his eyes had benefited from state aid while the dreams and hopes of his white community had been destroyed. The most revelatory and unsettling thing for Jeff Schoep was that he had no counter response to her points. He had no automatic response to cling to. He had not rehearsed this. How could the Black man and the immigrant have anything in common with the circumstances that he had endured? How could they share his hopes and aspirations? The space that was left, once the rhetoric could no longer cope with the questions being asked, was filled with doubt. That's when the cracks started to appear. If he couldn't answer using his armoury of stock responses, then perhaps there was some truth to what this Muslim woman was telling him. She had made such a simple comparison but delivered it with curiosity and care.

'There's nothing amazing in that conversation,' admitted Deeyah freely, though perhaps too modestly, 'other than just the willingness to really try to dig into some of this with each other. Doing it as you would with somebody that you care about. I think that's the difference.'

Some of these men held steadfastly to their beliefs, even though they accepted that she had approached them with a mixture of empathy and patience. At one point, one of them even said to her, 'I'm going to work against your world view till my last breath because I despise it, and I dislike it, and I disagree with it, but I respect the fact that you're very sincere.'

As well as the predictable pushback from some of the white supremacists, there were those within Deeyah's own social circle who objected vociferously to the very act of speaking to these people, wondering what it could possibly achieve. Her reaction to so many of those complaints will be deemed controversial by those who believe that very visible activism automatically elicits change. Also implicit in her statement below is a questioning of the motives behind such forms of protest. As a person holds their handmade placard aloft and takes care that the image of them holding it makes it onto their social media feeds, do they ever stop to ask themselves if such an act made any difference? A collective sense of empowerment, a communal gathering where catchy chants are formulated and repeated, a show of force against the enemy. All of these elements are laudable, but Deeyah was unflinching in her assessment of what her attendance at such events actually achieved: 'I've gone to all the anti-fascist marches, but it didn't accomplish anything other than me feeling really good about myself, and it does feel really good to be self-righteous, but it doesn't get you anywhere.'

There were worries that this documentary would normalise the attitudes and behaviour of racists, as well as giving them a platform and the free publicity they craved. What Deeyah intended, though, was to steer the conversation away from this well-trodden ground. In the process of making this documentary, it dawned on Deeyah that she had previously dismissed their humanity completely, and it became clear to her that no progress could be made – progress being defined as fewer Nazis in the world – if she continued to look at them with that mindset.

As I am sure you have figured out by now, this chapter is really about how we have to understand who we are and what burdens we carry before we can connect with someone from whom we are estranged. This is a book about having better conversations, but when it comes to having the really difficult ones, the work begins before you get close to the person whose views you cannot stomach. Awareness of our own emotions, assumptions and blind spots is crucial to navigating the difficult terrain of a challenging conversation. The stereotypes seared into your consciousness, the monoliths of your experience casting their shadows over your present, that righteous indignation that acts as a foundation for the moral framework that you exist within. Does 'cancelling' a Nazi ensure that there is one less Nazi in the world to worry about? Yes, according to some. But that was not the solution as far as Deeyah Khan was concerned.

I asked her if she was interviewing these men or having a conversation with them. It was a rhetorical question as I already knew what her answer would be, having watched the documentary. The interviewer gives little of themselves as the purpose of the meeting is to concentrate on the interviewee. But a difficult dialogue must involve something akin to a bartering of ideas, emotions and experiences. Both sides must possess what the other one needs; in that dynamic, a trade-off happens that leaves both parties satisfied with the outcome. That cannot happen if one side does not need what the other is offering. For Deeyah to ask for a glimpse of their humanity, she would have to offer up to them a glimpse of her own. 'I feel I can't ask someone to come out and put themselves on the line and be really vulnerable if I'm not willing to do the same, so I would very consciously also share things about my life with them.'

I wondered if Deeyah had a toolkit that she drew on to help her build successful connections. She explained, 'I do a lot of research, but I almost never have prepared questions. I try to listen to what somebody is saying and I follow them. I go where I'm curious and where they're going as well. I'm sincerely curious. I genuinely want to know what they have to say.'

The answer Deeyah gave me reflected my own approach to both conversation and the interview process, with curiosity being the key component. However, as I sit here and go through the transcripts of the conversations I had with these two inspirational women about their experiences of crossing the divide, I wouldn't want you to think that this is a rigid template to adhere to in every situation. It is more about the feelings that these people brought to their encounters than it is a list of instructions for how to mend the broken relationships in your life. The reason I got in contact with these people was because they represent what is possible and what is achievable in the most onerous situations. The inherent difficulty of crossing a divide or mending a broken relationship is not to be underestimated. Each situation must be approached with the openness and curiosity employed by the people you have just read about. Without these two attributes, finding common ground would be an arduous, if not impossible task. As you have already noted, it also takes a level of self-awareness that allows someone to identify their own prejudices and focus on how those sensibilities could derail any meaningful connection. Everyone must find their own way to have a conversation across the divide, though I do believe that real understanding only comes when the situation is approached with self-knowledge and an open mind.

In 2020, Deeyah made a film called *America's War on Abortion*. During the course of filming, she was confronted by a group of anti-abortionists who were demonstrating outside an abortion clinic, screaming abuse at people entering the building. They then turned on the Asian film-maker with the camera, threatening her with rape and calling her a terrorist. But it was when one of them looked Deeyah directly in the eyes and said, 'You cut the clit off your baby!' that Deeyah, in her words, 'actually lost it'. The police were called and a situation that could have escalated very quickly was defused.

Almost immediately, Deeyah realised that her reaction was exactly what they wanted. The anger that had swelled up within her had to subside for there to be any dialogue. As a film-maker, she had to go back and speak to the very people who had been so vile to her. Tempers had cooled off, though the insults that had been fired at her still hung in the air. And yet Deeyah was still able to make an assessment that many would find it hard to arrive at in that moment, or indeed afterwards: 'Even when they behave like that, that is not the entirety of who they are.' This didn't mean she was accepting their views, though – 'That doesn't mean you give the shittiness of who they are a pass. You're just acknowledging that that's not the entirety of a human being.' As with the white supremacists, Deeyah was not willing to see the anti-abortionists entirely as the sum of their views, even after such extreme provocations. However, a conversation still needed to be had to find that other side of who they were, the one that lay under the surface of their beliefs. 'I try really, really hard to speak to that side. To invite that part of them out, because if I can do that, that's where it becomes productive.'

Have you ever tried to convince someone that your side of the argument is the right one? Has it ended up as a heated exchange? Have voices been raised, temperatures risen and fallouts occurred? At the end of it, did you accomplish what you wanted to? Once the shouting stopped, had the person with an opposing view shifted towards your position or had you both just dug in and doubled down? I am assuming the latter, unless you are the boss of a company and your employees always defer to your unimpeachable wisdom out of respect, and a fear of losing their jobs. In a world where certain circumstances, such as politics and religion, dictate that some relationships are destined to be poisoned before they even begin, I wondered how it felt when you could finally see that the antidote was slowly working and the toxins that had prevented any chance of there being a relationship began to dissipate. I asked Deeyah what it was like when she began to see someone's hate fall away before her eyes through the act of having a conversation with them. She began by saying how disorientating it was. It was almost unbelievable because the views being espoused by neo-Nazis or anti-abortionists were so strongly held, how could they possibly wish to engage with those who they had dehumanised? It's true that not all did, but some did, and by identifying them, singling them out and spending time with them, progress was made. 'Conversations can only happen in an intimate space, it can't happen in big groups,' Deeyah observed.

Towards the end of our time together, Deeyah readily

admitted to not believing that her modus operandi would guarantee results. These conversations not only changed those whom she spoke to, but they also surprised her in ways that would have been unimaginable just a few years before. 'If you would've said to me a couple of years ago, the three of them are going to leave [the neo-Nazi organisations they were part of] and you're even going to become friends with some of them, I would've been offended that you could think that about me.'

And that is the most life-enhancing aspect of the multi-award-winning documentary that Deeyah Khan made. A Muslim, female, brown-skinned film-maker became friends with men who were, on first meeting, unapologetic white supremacists. After spending time with her and seeing the person that she was, and not the person they assumed her to be, some of these soon-to-be former racists decided that they no longer wanted to be a part of the organisations that still saw people like her as the enemy. Though Deeyah is keen not to oversimplify what happened to her. She fully admits that what she experienced was not a universal template for eradicating racism from the world, and that she had not simply eradicated any judgements of them and their attitudes from her mind. 'I'm not going to pretend like I don't have judgements of racists,' admitted Deeyah, 'but I try not to sit there and blame and condemn and keep the judgement at the forefront of how I'm engaging with somebody.'

In making *White Right: Meeting the Enemy*, Deeyah Khan had to overcome her own judgements and fears, place herself in harm's way and show extraordinary levels of patience. Her modesty as we drew our conversation to a close was misplaced. Yes, the reasons why racism exists in some places and flourishes within some groups are complex. And while talking to your detractors may just be one element of the process of making sure the world has one less racist in it, it is such a vital one. The achievement of that is a testament to the power of talking: 'All I've learned from this is that there are multiple levels on which we need to tackle racism and this is just one more tool; conversation is just one more tool. Look at conflict-resolution people, that's what they do all the time.'

Which brings me on nicely to my next example of how we can overcome the most difficult of scenarios by employing the words that are in our heads. Using them wisely, judiciously and at all times being open, curious and empathetic. Although this time with a structure, formal training and the knowledge that if it goes wrong, lives will immediately be put at risk.

9

John Sutherland:
Lessons from a Hostage Negotiator

I feel truly blessed to have had the opportunity to be a part of so many insightful conversations over the years on the radio shows and podcasts I host. The people who agree to tell their stories and sometimes relive their traumas are quite simply some of the bravest people that I have ever met. So many of my guests have recounted their battles with a whole range of addictions, traumatising experiences at the hands of an abuser or the debilitating effects of coping with severe mental health challenges. Then there are those who managed to escape torture and repression in their homelands and eventually found sanctuary in a country that doesn't deny them their basic human rights. They all carry the physical and psychological scars of what they have been through.

Throughout the course of a year, my listening audience will be presented with a wide spectrum of human experiences, from the most uplifting and joyous to an exploration of some of the darkest aspects of our nature. As I sit and listen while they recount these stories, it has crossed my mind more than once to wonder how it is that they have come to be here in front of me, having endured so much. The fact that they agree to enter a studio and talk about these life-altering moments, allowing people like me to ask them probing questions about what happened, only increases the respect that I have for them all. Without exception, they want aspects of their history to be told so that others can know what evil humans can do, but also to make sense of a world that contains both concentrated evil and selfless heroism. Even the most graphically upsetting and challenging conversations I have end with hope.

In the course of these interactions, I encourage but never cajole the person in front of me to bare their soul. People in my line of work should always endeavour to make sure that this is an invitation to open up but never an excuse to be either voyeuristic or salacious. When an experienced presenter gets that wrong, it suggests that their goal is to grab headlines and make a name for themselves, rather than act as a conduit for a person to shape their own narrative, in their own time. As with all invitations, the invitee has a right to decline the offer to speak. Just because they have a book to sell or a documentary to promote, that commercial transaction should not distract from the fact that these are lived experiences.

I am often asked about how difficult it is to conduct interviews such as these. The truth is that I relish them. Not because I want to see people upset, but because they

are difficult conversations and navigating them successfully is a challenge, but one that has the potential to bring
meaningful reward. It requires research, patience and a
willingness to listen. Of course, any disquiet I may feel
pales into insignificance in comparison to the emotional
fortitude needed to repeat some of the darkest moments
imaginable. My job is to give space and autonomy to
someone who has granted me the honour of an audience
with them. If they are on the verge of tears and feel the
need to pause to gather their thoughts, that time is not my
gift to give, it is their right. The temptation to jump in to
fill the silence, or what we call in radio 'dead air', should
be resisted. Those emotions must be allowed to rise and
overflow, or the interview may be paused momentarily to
let the feelings slowly dissipate.

The common misconception is that my role as an interviewer is to ask a list of pre-prepared questions; what
actually happens is that after the first question, the conversation is led by the interviewee's answers, with each
answer eliciting a question based on what I have just
heard. Nothing written down. Just a bank of knowledge
to draw upon and a conversation that could go anywhere.
The emotions may be raw and the subject matter challenging, but the terms of the exchange are that there is
a quid pro quo nature to the relationship. Most of what
I do takes place in a space that is designed to facilitate
communication from a technical perspective – the studio
setting means we can broadcast what is said to anyone
who chooses to listen, but it may inhibit normalcy and

openness due to that very environment. Microphones, screens and cameras surround me and while that may intimidate someone who is new to being interviewed, if I am doing my job correctly and helping my guest to feel at ease, the presence of cold technology should seem to melt away. What is left is two people talking. With sensitivity and, I hope, good grace, we can pause or even stop if it is necessary to do so. If someone felt that they could not carry on, or I could see how distressed they were, their microphone would be faded down. There may be a complaint if a listener feels that I have been insensitive (this hasn't happened yet) or rude (this usually happens when I grow tired of a politician not answering a very simple question), but other than on these rare occasions, the show must, and does, go on.

However, when I make eye contact with someone for whom life has been a series of near-catastrophic traumas, I know that they are not in the midst of crisis. By the time they arrive at my door, they are, on the whole, ready and able to talk about the past and process how that history has shaped their present and the ramifications for the future. For all the ebbs and flows of a broadcasting career that has clocked up thousands of hours of on-air time and involved so many sensitive conversations, I have never been placed in a situation that is ongoing and is so high-stakes that a breakdown in communication could lead to fatalities. It would be inconceivable that I'd find myself being asked to run towards an incident that everyone else was fleeing from in order to conduct an interview. I may have had to, on occasion, work hard to dilute a person's natural resistance to being interviewed. A reticence to engage may come from previous interviews that have gone badly or a creative who just wants the art to speak for itself and not have to explain it. I do not need to battle to win the trust of someone whose default position is in opposition to who I am and what in their eyes I stand for. The difficult conversations I have had would never take place in a situation where both me and the other person could potentially be in danger. If my radio show leaves the confines of a studio, to do what is known as an outside broadcast, risk assessments are completed and forms filled in by my production team way in advance of my arrival. My interviewing skills would never require me to be at the top of a building trying to coax someone back from a ledge or on a bridge in the early hours of the morning attempting to persuade a stranger that life is worth living.

For former Metropolitan Police Borough Commander and Chief Superintendent John Sutherland, this was his job. As a police negotiator, he received formal training in the art of talking people down, forming a connection and using a learned skill set to defuse very difficult situations. After retiring from the Metropolitan Police Service on medical grounds in 2018, he became a very successful author. His debut book *Blue* was a *Sunday Times* best-seller and, on a personal level, he is genuinely one of the nicest men you could ever meet. I am fascinated by how the training that he had received made him better suited to communicate with the world around him and I wanted to know how transferable those skills are to everyday life. Hence the reason I believed he would be able to provide an invaluable contribution to this book.

The absolute foundation of this book is that I believe that all of us can learn to be much better at talking and listening to our fellow humans. We have looked at how this can be done through being open-minded and open-hearted enough to engage with those around you. But what if there is a deeper level to how we speak with each other? A process that refines our actions and makes us more considered in what we say, how we say it and how effectively we receive the speech of others. I wanted to sit down and speak to someone for whom, in a professional context, every word has to be assessed before being uttered. We all quite often hear a string of words from an expert orator that could be said to be life-affirming; in the scenarios that you are about to be presented with, the role of words is life-saving.

I began my conversation by asking John about the basic building blocks that are needed in order to be a police crisis negotiator. There is always a pause before he speaks and you are immediately struck by how thoughtful he is. His voice radiates warmth and an almost meditative tone; as he spoke to me, I had no doubt as to how good he must have been at his job. 'Broadly, there are two approaches to negotiating. Firstly, there's the highly technical one, where you've got people who are quite scientific in their approach. Secondly, there's a much more instinctive approach that is based more on empathy and instinct.'

Having spoken to John before and read his books, I already knew that he fell into the latter category more than the former, but it was evident that in order to be effective as a police negotiator you would need to be able to have a perspective and a focus that combined both approaches. He describes himself as instinctively an empath, which is why he was drawn to the role in the first place. But even more fundamental than that is the 'concern for humanity' that he possesses. This was vital in his role, but actually it is something we should all aspire to have within our armoury of character traits if we are to get the best out of the relationships we have in this world. A concern for those around us shouldn't be dismissed as being 'snowflakey' or lead to accusations of being a 'social justice warrior', which has bizarrely become a term of abuse, as if fighting for social justice is somehow a thing to be mocked and derided.

Police officers often have to deal with criminal actions that can be the result of a poor education, scant mental health provision, poverty, neglect and a paucity of opportunity. For John Sutherland, at that moment when his skills were called upon to de-escalate a sensitive situation, his focus was on the person or persons in crisis. While the basis of being a good conversationalist is being a good listener, in a negotiating context, the terminology and the skills required go way beyond just being a friendly face and a shoulder to cry on. 'It's all about what negotiators call "active listening". It's not just about passively not speaking, it's actively listening, not just to what you're saying but how you're saying it.'

Have you ever found yourself drifting off as a colleague, friend or relative begins to speak? In that situation, ask yourself if you are fully involved in the conversation or simply using silence to mask your disinterest. I found our conversation so fascinating because it was the first time I'd consciously thought about not just what the person opposite me was saying but how they were saying it. After the sheer amount of time that I have spent in front of a microphone conversing for a living, I am, of course, subconsciously processing when my interlocutor's eyes expand or contract, the expressions their mouth makes as I speak, how their eyebrows rise or fall and whether their brow furrows or remains smooth. None of these movements necessarily affect what my next question may be. At times, I will have to press on, albeit gently, even if I see that a question or comment has been misinterpreted or been challenging in a way the recipient has found unsettling. The police negotiator has to be mindful of the potentially dire consequences if a cue is missed, an action overlooked or a non-verbal plea ignored. For a man or woman doing this job, being alert to the minutiae of movements the human body makes is an imperative. The former police officer was at pains to emphasise how important this aspect of the role is. 'It's about reading your non-verbals as well as your verbals. I'm all on receive rather than transmit.'

As with Mary McAleese and Deeyah Khan, building trust is key and, as we know, that takes time, patience and a willingness to engage. The major difference is that, for people like John Sutherland, time is never on their side. I wonder if either the former president of Ireland or the documentary film-maker was ever so consciously aware of the non-verbal signifiers they were being presented with as they attempted to build bridges across what had once seemed unbridgeable gulfs.

John broke down some of the different scenarios an officer in his position is presented with. When the person you are trying to pacify is most likely paralysed by fear themselves, a calm demeanour and finely tuned set of objectives are what is needed. As John described these scenarios to me, I was struck by how utterly terrified I would be if placed in such situations. Think for a moment about what you would do if tasked with asking someone to relinquish a knife or any other weapon that they were going to use to injure themselves or others. Try to picture how you would act when imploring someone in crisis to step back from the edge high above the streets. Could you remain calm when negotiating with a man whose face you cannot see, trying to gauge his mental state, knowing that behind the closed door of the family home, he is holding those he is supposed to love and protect hostage and threatening to hurt them? For the men and women who decide to take on the role of a crisis negotiator, this is the reality of their everyday working lives and honing their communication skills is a vital component of being effective.

John is adamant that the receiving of information trumps the transmitting of instructions. He put the entire basis of the job into three words: 'It is all about empathy, rapport and trust.' He paused and I could see that something had popped into his mind that he simply had to share. He asked me if I had ever seen or ever heard anyone talk about the Chinese symbol for listening. I said that I hadn't, but I am so glad John's question gave me the prompt to learn about it as it is absolutely fascinating.

聽

The character, which is believed to be over 2,000 years old, is a lesson to all about the importance of adhering to ancient wisdom when trying to understand our twenty-first century world. The pictogram that the Chinese refer to as 'ting' breaks down into four quadrants. In the top left corner of the symbol we have the ears (to hear). The top right of the quad explains that we have the eyes (to see). So far, so obvious, but then it begins to get interesting, as the top right and bottom right of the quadrant are divided by a symbol that simply instructs you to give your undivided attention to the person that is talking. The bottom right quad explains that you have to employ your heart to feel, which is the empathy that John spoke of, and in the bottom left corner of the symbol, you are asked to use your mind to think about what the person who is speaking to you is actually trying to verbalise. Without understanding of the importance of all of these parts and putting into practice the instructions the symbol gives us, you are unlikely to derive what you really need from an exchange of ideas, experiences or emotions.

So ask yourself if you are really listening when someone is talking. Is your attention undivided? Are you employing the full range of emotions at your disposal to connect with what you are hearing? Are you looking at that person as well as listening to them, noticing the physiological movements that thoughts divulge before speech clarifies?

What John's example also shows us is that we now attach a very narrow definition to the idea of listening. 'It seems to me that the Chinese had understood something about listening that the limitations of the English language doesn't quite capture. It's about your eyes and your heart, even your soul.' Bear in mind that this man isn't regurgitating a series of new-age practices gleaned from a two-week yoga retreat. He is describing the elements needed in order to be an effective police negotiator. His training wasn't designed to exist in computer modelling and role-play exercises. There is no abstraction in relation to real-world human crises. In so many cases, John has often had just hours to apply the knowledge he has in order to defuse and de-escalate.

I asked John what happens when a sequence of increasingly alarming events has led to a very dangerous situation, one that requires police involvement – what are those all-important first words you say to someone on the brink of hurting themselves or others? But then I realised that perhaps the question itself is a naïve one. Could there really be one script that is valid for every potential problem? I asked. John gave a knowing smile and an almost inaudible chuckle at this point. Not because he was being callous or had become so world-weary, but because there is a widely known almost-mantra employed by those engaged in negotiating in such perilous circumstances. He told me that any other negotiators listening into our conversation would also raise a wry smile. 'You are taught that pretty much every negotiation begins with exactly the same phrase: My name is John. I'm with the police. And I'm here to help you.'

The two of us then began to role-play as I tried to imagine what it would be like to be an angry man who sees no hope in the world and wants the pain to end. My response to John's calm and considered statement was fuelled by confusion, pain, anger, fear and poor acting.

NA: 'Fuck off, I don't want your help!'
JS: 'You sound angry . . .'
NA: 'I am fucking angry. I don't want you here. I hate this life. I'm going to kill myself.'
JS: 'I don't want you to do that, Nihal. Tell me why you're angry.'
NA: 'Everything. Money. My ex. My job. Nothing's worth it. No one cares about me, no one gives a shit.'
JS: 'I give a shit. Tell me about . . .'

At this juncture, I noted the tone of John's voice, how calm it was, considering the real-world scenarios in which he would have used similar words in the past. It was also devoid of judgement. He used words sparingly. He didn't over-elaborate or resort to hyperbole, but made sure every word mattered and had a purpose. Though in this case he was only faced with my terrible attempts at amateur dramatics, his approach was to constantly assess the difficulties before him while remaining positive about the outcome.

In his time as a police negotiator, John covered somewhere between thirty and fifty negotiations of different types. Of all of those cases, only one ended with a bad outcome. That outcome being the death of the thirty-two-year-old barrister Mark Saunders, who was shot dead by police marksmen in May 2008 after officers feared that he was about to fire his shotgun at them. The transcript of John's interaction with the victim is available to read online and I encourage you to take a look. There was an inquest into the police shooting of Mr Saunders in 2010 and afterwards, out of respect for the man's family, John made a promise to never speak in public about the events that took place in Markham Square again. But having read the transcript of the series of exchanges between Mr Saunders and John, I was struck by how calm, empathetic and gently inquiring he was.

The details of that day are as follows: there is a man who appears to be in his own home, has been drinking heavily and is in turns terrified, angry and upset; he also has a loaded shotgun at his disposal. The Chinese symbol for listening and all its constituent parts was employed fully here as John clearly used his ears to listen to every word, answer every question and suggest a more positive alternative to any doomsday option which a deeply vulnerable man expressed. In engaging his mind and heart to work together, that essential bond of trust was constructed with each sentence. At all times, John remained optimistic.

Even though the transcript does not include the words that Mr Saunders said to John Sutherland, who was the senior police negotiator on site, you can safely assume from John's responses that the man on the other end of the phone was incredibly troubled by many aspects of his life. From 6.58 p.m., when John first left a voicemail message on Mark Saunders' mobile phone, then twelve minutes later as they make contact at around 7.10 p.m. and the dialogue begins, to the point at which armed officers open fire at approximately 9.31 p.m., Mark Saunders felt vulnerable and endangered, but to the police and public, he was a potentially dangerous individual that they needed protection from. The transcript makes clear that Mr Saunders spoke to John about many things. Their discourse covered his meetings with a therapist, the undoubted love he had for his wife, his seeming willingness to use his gun and the fear that he had that he would be shot dead that day by the police. He must have also talked about killing himself.

In 2010, while the inquest was still ongoing, a *Daily Mail* journalist wrote a piece that asked robust questions about the police response with a headline that read: 'Yes he was armed, drunk and deranged. But wasn't it overkill for seven officers to shoot dead Mark Saunders?' In this article, which, as you may have already gathered, was critical of the police actions that fateful day, the reporter changed tack from criticism to praise when writing about Superintendent John Sutherland's involvement as the lead police crisis negotiator: 'I was moved by Mr Sutherland's quiet, persistent decency and his attempts to reassure Mr Saunders.' Those reassurances sadly did not produce the desired outcome and a man was shot dead by the police. As the conversation arrived at Saunders' death, John's voice quietened and his mood changed. 'That will be with me for the rest of my life,' he simply said.

Throughout that evening, the most vital emotion of all was optimism. Negotiators, like good conversationalists, have to be optimists. The most powerful driver in achieving a positive outcome must be optimism. It is hope that focuses the mind, overcomes the negativity and powers the strategy that has life-saving at its core. On the part of the negotiator, it is a mix of personality and experience that shapes a belief that what you are presented with will end up with a positive outcome.

Whenever John speaks to an assembled group of would-be police negotiators at the Metropolitan Police's training school in north London, he always tells them that, no matter what, 'Never, ever forfeit your humanity.' This is someone in need of help. That person may well be armed, unpleasant and potentially violent, but if the trained officer no longer sees them as a person and solely as a criminal, then the situation could get a whole lot worse.

LET'S TALK

You may consider yourself to be an empathetic individual because you stop to speak to a rough sleeper and have various direct debits distributing a manageable portion of your income to charities, but what if your capacity for empathy was challenged by someone who you didn't believe was deserving of it? It would seem that, increasingly, there are those who take pride in projecting out into the world how hard-headed and devoid of empathy they are, seeing the world through a lens of emotional protectionism which barricades itself off from the need to imagine how it would feel to be placed in a precarious situation. It is a mindset that resolutely refuses to acknowledge a shared humanity, preferring to create a more insular world. If a boat full of desperate people seeking a better life capsizes and men, women and children die at sea, their default position is to find ways to blame the victims, the system, the traffickers, but they never consider what prompted people to take such risks in the first place. It is an attitude I find difficult to connect with and yet I must attempt to discover the root of those opinions. Even though I may find their views unsavoury and notice how much they contrast with my own values, simply refusing to engage with those who think like this will yield little in the way of expanding my own understanding of the world we live in. The police crisis negotiator, too, must extinguish their own judgements and prejudices from the process. It is a point that John was keen to make. 'Some of the people you deal with are deeply unpleasant. Most of the people you deal with, though, are just deeply broken.'

The Hollywood version of hostage negotiating relies on a bank heist going very wrong and a masked felon hijacking a car, putting a gun to the driver's head and trying to violently negotiate his way out of a perilous predicament. We've probably all seen a movie where international terrorists are in control of a skyscraper full of terrified employees and law enforcement is attempting to talk them down, employing a lot of carrots while planning to use a lot of sticks. These films are full of big dramatic scenes, involving hostages, bloodthirsty villains and guns blazing. The reality is smaller, more intimate and personal. These are human crises that could lead to human crimes, but the emphasis is on the crisis, in the first instance, in order to hopefully prevent the situation escalating to tragedy.

Put yourself in this scenario: you have been asked to attend an ongoing situation at a care home. An elderly man is sat in a chair in the middle of the communal lounge with a knife in his hand that he is holding to his own throat. He is threatening to kill himself. The reason for this uncharacteristic outburst is love. He has fallen for another resident and sadly for him his feelings have not been reciprocated. What would you do to prevent this septuagenarian from hurting and perhaps even killing himself? Following John's advice, start by introducing yourself, tell him your job and that you are here to help. Let him tell you his story. How he came to be in this predicament. He is angry, agitated. The setting seems so incongruous to the drama that is unfolding within it, but that shouldn't distract you. Take a calculated risk by shifting the attention away from the man's own self-loathing and point that energy towards the object of his affection. Make her out to be the villain of the piece as John Sutherland did. This may backfire, incur his wrath and lead to him doing exactly what you do not want him to do. Continue undaunted by the doubts in your head. Believe in your instinct and training. Ask him why he should give someone, who clearly doesn't like him, the satisfaction of knowing that he is going to hurt himself. Speak slowly, it will give you time to search for clues in his behaviour that will help you know what to do next. Make sure your head isn't so full of unnecessary words that you are prevented from listening to his. The strategy of asking him not to play into her hands by harming himself works and there is a breakthrough. How do you think you would have fared when presented with a crisis such as this? For John Sutherland, it was 'one of the most poignantly memorable negotiations I ever dealt with'.

John's training enables him to have better conversations in all areas of his life. He uses the skills he learned from his job every day as a husband and a father. 'It's all about communication. It's all about empathy. It's all about active listening. It's all about rapport. It's all about building trust.' Always ask open questions which begin with a 'what', 'where', 'why' or 'when' because you want the person in front of you to open up and not give them the opportunity to bluntly answer with a 'yes' or a 'no'. Secondly, be aware of reacting in a way that is encouraging; the police call these 'minimal encourages' and they include things like maintaining eye contact, nodding and verbal cues that signal that you are listening and fully engaged. There is also a term 'emotional labelling'. This means that rather than reacting directly to a statement made or an angry question, you react to the emotion underpinning the words and simply say, 'You sound really upset. You sound really angry. Tell me about that.' This aims to deflect attention away from what they are saying towards why they are saying it and builds the relationship through a genuine interest in how the person in crisis is feeling.

I hope that you will never have to employ these tactics in the kind of situations that John has found himself in, but there is trauma all around us. You may encounter a rough sleeper who, more than anything else, wants someone to talk to at that moment. There may be a person within your friendship group or family experiencing their own mental health challenges. Perhaps you are needed as a shoulder to cry on as your friend's relationship breaks down. You can't fix it. You don't have the solution. But you have ears to listen with and a voice to gently coax out of them how they are feeling.

John explained some of the techniques and possible responses we may have if placed in any of the predicaments outlined above. One of these techniques is called 'echoing'. He asked me to make a statement. As I looked beyond my computer screen and out of my window at the all-too familiar grey skies for what seemed like the hundredth day in a row, I simply said, 'The weather in

Manchester is horrendous all the time,' to which John calmly responded, 'All the time?' It is a technique that is designed to draw me back into the conversation by using the last word or phrase that I used. It further reinforces to the speaker that John is listening to them, but it also, as John said, 'puts the ball straight back in your court'. I have to respond and it opens me up to further explore the factually inaccurate but emotionally draining statement I have just made about Greater Manchester's climate. It, above all else, keeps the conversation going.

Another tool is that of 'a presupposition'. It is about subtly placing a positive outcome in the mind of 'someone who's feeling very fatalistic in the most literal sense'. What if you are in phone contact but cannot see the person who is both a danger to himself and those around him? This man wants to tell the negotiator that he must speak to a loved one and say goodbye to them. For any trained police negotiator, this is immediately a 'flashing red light'. You cannot give the man any opportunity to say good-bye while he is still a danger to himself and others. The goodbye this man wants to have a chance to say has a finality attached to it that goes beyond the breakdown of a relationship. He isn't saying goodbye to just one person but potentially to life itself. So you presuppose a positive outcome. Once verbalised, this becomes an invitation to the person on the end of the phone to imagine a differ-ent future. As John pointed out to Mark Saunders that evening, 'Once you are out, the first thing that you can do is talk to her.' It goes back to the negotiator's fundamental requirement to be optimistic. It presupposes that the man in question has already dropped his weapon, that he will realise that what he actually wants is to live, to survive this ordeal and to find a way back from the darkness that is enveloping him at that moment.

However much of an optimist you may be, though, you are not naïve, therefore you will be presupposing that the least worst outcome is within arm's reach, and that is not to be mistaken for describing it as the best outcome. None of the participants will be left entirely unscarred by the incident. Even if everyone survives, someone may be successfully prosecuted, and those at the very core of the incident may well be traumatised for a long time by what they have experienced.

One of the most striking things that John said to me was at the very beginning of our conversation. It related to the very first exercise he was asked to do when he was being assessed for his suitability to become a negotiator. In this scenario, the police negotiator is asked to go to the house of a colleague who has not arrived at work that day. You are placed on one side of the door and you have to talk to the colleague on the other side of the door. Faced with this situation, John explained that he had to separate in a very fundamental way the negotiator from the police officer, because the latter is 'by instinct and training a problem-solver. You go into situations wanting to fix them. Negotiating is the antithesis of that. Negotiation is not about fixing a problem. Negotiation is about building a relationship. And so what I said in that selection exercise was less important than what I heard and what I did with what I heard.'

Throughout this section, we have learned from those who are not seeking to solve a problem but to build a bridge. Even in the case of Mary McAleese, as while the objective was to build a lasting peace and to get the paramilitaries to renounce violence, the negotiators did not approach those initial conversations with an agenda bolted onto them. You will recall that they initially talked about anything but the serious problems they faced, because they knew that creating a bond of trust was the most important thing of all. When film-maker Deeyah Khan travelled to America and sat in front of the neo-Nazis with a camera pointed at them, she didn't see these men as a problem that she needed to solve, or indeed could solve. She wanted to try to understand how they had come to be that way, so she set about asking them questions, but also giving something of herself so that it was a genuine dialogue. The formal training John Sutherland received from London's Metropolitan Police codified that which was already a part of him, namely empathy and curiosity.

These three have shown how, when having difficult conversations, the best approach is one of patience and a genuine desire to understand – but not justify or excuse – views that are diametrically opposed to your own. What drives those opinions? Are those drivers actually shared ones but with different outcomes? Does there exist any common ground that you can both inhabit? Once the superficialities and the generalisations are stripped away and people are no longer wholly identified by a single characteristic, whether that be skin colour, sexual orientation or religion, it is possible to find a deeper connection.

I hosted a phone-in show on the BBC Asian Network before I joined BBC Radio 5 Live and over the years I had countless conversations with members of my audience in which a man or woman would share how their family no longer spoke to them because they had married someone from a different culture or religion. I remember once a woman telling me that her parents had a picture of every single grandchild on proud display in their house, except for her kids, who, because she had married someone from a different caste, were not deemed to be worthy of being put on show in a frame. It is difficult to understand how parents can place their own cultural markers above the happiness of their children. How they can punish their own grandchildren in such a way. If terrorists can become peacemakers, neo-Nazis can renounce their former beliefs and a crisis negotiator can use the power of words to prevent someone from killing themselves, then these familial disagreements can be overcome. Through dialogue and a willingness to engage with open ears, eyes, mind and heart, a recognition of your own prejudices, an understanding that you cannot simply fix the problem and the patience to see how the situation develops, perhaps you can use what you have read here to mend something that you once regarded to be unrepairable.

PART 4

CONVERSATIONS IN THE WORKPLACE

10

Let's Talk About Jobs

Take your attention away from this book for a few moments and transport yourself back through a timeline of all your previous jobs. Start with your first job as a teenager and proceed from there. Do your muscles remember the achingly mundane motions that accompanied hours of robotically stacking shelves in a supermarket; the delicate balancing of plates along your entire arm while waiting tables in a restaurant; or nodding politely to the regulars as you pulled pints behind the bar hoping that it wouldn't kick off that night? As the opportunities to dodge the world of full-time work shrank, formal education drew to a close and the realisation dawned on you that you would have to become an actual grown-up, try to recollect the multitude of different people you met when you first entered full-time employment. When you were a junior, an intern, a rookie, who was your manager, their boss and then their superior? Who are the colleagues that even five, ten or twenty years later still stand out for having made an indelible impression on your memory?

As you flick through images of their faces in your mind, pass over the kind ones, the inspirational ones and the supportive workmates. Try to home in on an individual whom you have met in the world of work who you would describe as 'not being much of a people person'. This particular individual may have found themselves in a position of authority through opaque hiring practices that nobody could quite understand. They may not have possessed the requisite skills to be able to inspire and connect, but perhaps they found themselves in the role because the company valued stone-cold diligence over emotional intelligence. Or maybe this person just came from a generation which believed in the 'treat 'em mean, keep 'em keen/divide and rule' school of workplace efficiency and made no attempt to evolve. Or was it a combination of ruthless ambition and sycophancy that propelled them to an executive role? If neither cultural nor generational issues are to blame, perhaps these people, who we have all encountered at some point in our careers, were just parachuted into a high-level position through good old-fashioned nepotism.

In many workplaces, there will be that one person somewhere in the food chain of authority who is unable to conduct even the most basic of interactions with a colleague without coming across as rude and patronising. This is not in any way meant to be construed as a lack of understanding for neurodiversity in the workplace. A co-worker on the autism spectrum may find it difficult to process social cues in the same way as others and this can often be misinterpreted as being aloof or dismissive. It is always valuable for all concerned to remember that not all disabilities are visible. These are not the people that I am talking about. The ones that I want to focus on are unable to, or choose not to, see beyond the processes of a business and disregard how important it is to be able to talk with employees and colleagues. They hide behind rules and regulations, meetings and presentations, and fail to understand the value of genuine dialogue. These are the people who are so inept at interpersonal communication, so keen on the strictures of bureaucracy and so chained to jargon and corporate statutes that it's a wonder if they achieve anything without creating resentment.

Wherever they take place, conversations matter. Simple exchanges can transform an idea into a reality, bridge a gap in understanding or make a colleague feel valued and inspired. Ignoring the power of good dialogue will surely have a detrimental effect on how an organisation functions. Imagine a firm that has a rigid hierarchical structure, facilitating a vice-like grip on subordinates. Ordinances filter down from the boardroom to the executive and these missives then pass through various layers of management without explanation or encouragement. Try to imagine working in a business like this. If you are on the bottom rung of the corporate ladder, the one who has to do as they're told without consultation, collaboration or context, then there would seem to be little reason to feel invested in doing the job to the best of your abilities. If you are a business owner, you may be asking if such a company even exists beyond the realms of a Dickensian fable, and if it does, how long such an enterprise would survive in the modern world.

The reality is that many organisations, both large and small, still do not value or understand the benefits to be gained from spending time working on conversational skills within their businesses and the importance of making those on the payroll feel valued. For any business, analysing how people communicate with each other, and the quality of that communication, is essential. Using email chains and webinar sessions to spread information throughout an organisation has its place, but if it is the sole means of propagating ideas or confronting difficulties, then that is to the detriment of the endeavour.

These issues became even more pronounced once our working lives were completely transformed by an event that none of us could have foreseen. The coronavirus pandemic curtailed our ability to meet in person and changed working practices overnight. In a matter of days, people disappeared from office spaces as their living rooms, spare bedrooms and kitchen tables became their desks, meeting rooms and canteens. Everything became remote, restricted and distanced. For creative organisations in particular, this removal of person-to-person contact sucked the energy from the creative process. The founder of Netflix, Reed Hastings, put it succinctly when he told the *Wall Street Journal* in 2020 that he saw no positives in working from home as far as his business was concerned. He said, 'Not being able to get together in person, particularly internationally, is a pure negative.' But these unprecedented developments encouraged us to rethink old orthodoxies, with companies such as Twitter and Fujitsu going the other way and announcing that their staff could effectively work from home forever if they so wished.

As you would expect, there were differing opinions on the pros and cons of a new working reality. For the majority, the working week is Monday through until Friday; these are the days that, pre-pandemic, employers expected employees to be seen in their orthodox working environments of concrete, glass and steel. Working eight thirty to five – what a way to make a living. A request to WFH would have most likely been met with a WTF?! There was most certainly a stigma attached to working from home pre-2020, but over the course of numerous lockdowns, those views changed in a relatively short space of time.

In March 2021, three academics surveyed 5,000 British workers to discover what the future of working from home would look like. The economists asked the group if perceptions around working from home had changed among people that they knew. Of those who responded to this question, 76 per cent of them believed that perceptions had improved. In America, to illustrate the differences between a pre- and mid-pandemic working life, only 5 per cent of an employee's work time was spent at home pre-pandemic, but by the spring of 2020, that portion of work time spent at home had jumped to 60 per cent. Research conducted by the economists looked at whether working from home would stick around and what proportion of their working week employees would want to spend working away from home. The results showed that employees preferred just one day a week out of the office. On average, the respondents felt that they were 2 per cent more efficient when their traditional office surroundings were replaced by a home space. While this may seem like a small increase in efficiency, it is in contrast to how employers would have viewed how efficient their employees were when working from home pre-pandemic. So one of the biggest fears managers had had before the onslaught of Covid-19 – that of work-shy staff watching daytime television while living *la vida sofa* at home – was not entirely borne out by the anecdotal evidence.

A report by Catalyst, a worldwide non-profit organisation that advises companies on how to create more inclusive spaces for women, did some fascinating research into the benefits of remote working. Authored by Dr Tara Van Bommel, the Catalyst report surveyed 7,487 employees across the world to look at differences between those who were given various options of working remotely and those whose only option was to be office-based. Employees who were given the option to work from home or else-where were less likely to want to leave the company in the following twelve months and being given the choice of a more flexible working environment led to women with children being less likely to want to leave their job compared to women with a family who did not have that opportunity. Those surveyed felt, as a whole, more inno-vative more of the time.

Pre-pandemic, just requesting to be allowed to work from home two or more days a week could well have been met with stone-cold silence and even incredulous laugh-ter by many employers, but it was not unheard of and we need to be aware of the effects that remote working had on people before Covid struck. As we get used to and begin to expect to be given the flexibility to choose where we do our work, it is also important to remember the potential pitfalls of being away from an office envi-ronment when others aren't. Research conducted by the *Harvard Business Review* in 2017 found that in a work setting where some employees had the choice to work remotely while others remained in the office, the effect on the morale of those who had made the decision to spend some portion of the working week at home was stark. They often came to realise that decisions were being made without their consent on projects that they were involved in. It became evident that their workmates who remained in the office were more likely to conspire against them and to gossip about them behind their backs. It wasn't a case of 'out of sight, out of mind', but rather 'out of sight, let's put the boot in'. If members of staff feel that they are being treated in this way because they have chosen to adopt flexible working practices, then it is incumbent on their managers to ensure that physical absence from the office does not mean a worsening of career prospects.

There were, of course, those who found the reconfiguring of work during the pandemic to be a positive because they had previously found the daily commute and the office environment harmful to their personal well-being. Going forward, they should be supported to work in a way that does not lead to their mental and physical health deteriorating, especially as we still do not fully understand the mental health ramifications of the pandemic. There were also many who embraced the opportunity to reassess their work-life balance. They discovered that the previous model was not one worth returning to. For others, the future may encompass a flexible working schedule, which could mean that for two or three days a week, a living room, a café or a nice spot under a tree may be the place they choose in order to be productive, creative and fulfilled. If our working lives are going to be hybrid, then those left in charge have a responsibility to make sure that employees at home don't feel marooned on a lonely island of increasing irrelevance.

The *Harvard Business Review* research led to a number of solutions that managers could implement in the face of challenges presented by our shifting working practices. The most relevant one to the subject of this book was the reinstatement of the 'water-cooler moment' as a specific time in the diary for manager and managed to have a conversation that is unrelated to work, even if it is through a webcam. Although the screen may be split into nine separate boxes, just making that time to talk about the events and incidents that shape a life beyond work has tangible benefits. These moments of chit-chat fortify relationships, increase trust and potentially reduce the chances of the kind of Machiavellian office politics that can be found in working environments taking root and poisoning professional relationships.

But for this strategy to work, there has to be a genuine interest in, and knowledge of, the team. A clumsy Zoom call where children's names are forgotten, insincere or crude banter is exchanged and a senior colleague hogs the limelight will not have the desired outcome. Returning to the Catalyst study, the researchers were adamant that one of the key elements to making remote working a success is ensuring that those who manage remotely are trained in the art of empathy and inclusiveness. Bridging any potential disconnect between an office-based manager and someone working from home requires, of those tasked with managing, traits that are also desirable within the workplace, such as empathy and inclusiveness. With flexibility may also come feelings of isolation from time to time; this needs to be recognised. Even in the office, we cannot allow the space in our working day that is needed just to have a casual chat that may be unrelated to work to be constantly squeezed and regarded as a luxurious add-on; employers must acknowledge it as a vital part of a working day. Deadlines can be time- and soul-destroying. Realising your ambitions has the potential to be exhausting and singular in focus, but sharing moments with a colleague shouldn't be an afterthought.

Throughout my career, I have seen and been told about examples of poor communicators in positions of authority. In some cases, there seems to be an inability to engender a team spirit, which inevitability creates a gulf between management and employee. This results in the most valuable resource a company has, the people within it, feeling disconnected from the mission, and when disillusionment eventually settles in, morale plummets. There is no real substitute for being present and approachable – another mistake those higher up the management structure make. When looking at the various parts of our lives where the need to have meaningful conversations are most evident, the spaces we work in rank pretty highly.

When I worked in the music industry in the 1990s, I encountered individuals whose behaviour would not be tolerated now. There was a bluntness bordering on aggression and a survival instinct that built the resilience needed to carry on. As a music PR in my twenties, it was my job to go out and generate new business. Going into major record companies to secure new sources of revenue exposed me to people who knew the power structure and my place in it – i.e. pretty low down the pecking order.

Thankfully, I didn't experience any of the horror stories that so many, especially women, can attest to. My two bosses were starkly different people, but both were hard-working, principled and inspirational. What I did see, though, was the desire of some to prove their superiority by belittling others and in that game I was, on occasion, willing to play the role of the subordinate in order to seal the deal. That may come across as a weakness of spirit and a lack of self-respect and professional pride. But the reality of the times I was working in meant this was a necessity in order to survive in a business that was relatively easy to get into but very difficult to stick at and prosper in. To work as a PR in the music industry, a sharpness was required because you had to deliver time and time again. You couldn't turn up to a record company meeting in their imposing offices and make excuses for a lack of progress in getting an artist the exposure they needed in order to be commercially viable.

When I look back on my career in the music industry, I can certainly identify times when I was unkind to people that I worked with. To my eternal shame, there were moments of abrasiveness and an inability to hide my frustration with a perceived lack of diligence. In my twenties, I mirrored some of the behaviours that I had seen around me and thought that that was the attitude to have in order to progress in an industry that was as ruthless as it was rewarding. I didn't necessarily see then that making others feel inferior was also a sign of insecurity and a need to feel superior, which is pathetic and counterproductive.

My first boss, and a mentor to this day, taught me so much and helped me to build myself a suit of armour to deal with the machinations of the music business, and life. He is an extremely successful record company executive and serial entrepreneur and he still inspires me. This is why even though I am afforded a certain degree of security by working in the public sector, the people who run businesses fascinate me. Those who take much bigger risks, have far more job insecurity and whose working lives seem so much more relentless have to ensure that while they are constantly having to adapt and evolve, they do not fail to nurture and develop the people who help their companies survive and thrive. What can we learn from their experiences of effective and ineffective conversational practice when it comes to managing people in order to prosper in our own endeavours? Are there just good bosses and bad ones, and you have to cope with the bad ones by simply soaking up their idiosyncrasies, bad manners and poor communication skills? What if all captains of industry could be better at communicating? If that were the case, then that culture of openness and adaptability would cascade down through the firm. Having spent just a few years in private business before joining the BBC, perhaps I am not best placed to advise corporate entities on how to create a better working environment through having better conversations, but as a former trustee of two of the world's largest public institutions, the

British Council and the Southbank Centre in London, I can say that I have witnessed the private sector from an entry-level vantage point and two venerable public bodies from the boardroom.

11

Rick Haythornthwaite:
Lessons from a CEO

The majority of the quarterly board meetings that took place in the level-five function room of the Southbank Centre, with its stunning views of the London Eye and County Hall as a backdrop, were chaired by the former Chair Rick Haythornthwaite. The tables were arranged in a giant square and every trustee was given the space to be able to express themselves without feeling like they were on trial. With the natural light flooding in and Royal Festival Hall just metres from us, every one of those meeting made me feel important.

My and Rick's paths had previously crossed while I was still on the board of the British Council, which is the world's largest public diplomacy organisation, tasked with promoting English language and British culture globally. When he became chair of the Southbank Centre, Rick and the then artistic director, Jude Kelly CBE, encouraged me to join the board. I had never encountered a man like Rick before. I had, of course, met men who were white-haired, smartly dressed and incredibly well educated before, but it was the way he chaired a meeting so effortlessly and productively that made such an impression on me; it was a masterclass in conversation, delegation and inspiration. He exuded a calm confidence that immediately made anyone in his orbit feel that they were the planet that would benefit most from his sunlight.

The people who gathered to discuss broader strategy were no joke. Like some Arthurian Round Table of corporate success, in each chair sat a titan of a private business, a CEO of a powerful company or an expert in the various elements needed to hold an executive to account. These specialists ranged from property developers to lawyers and even included a celebrated concert cellist. Even though at first I felt like a clown, Rick encouraged me to recognise my worth in that august company and grow into the role.

A book about conversations would not be complete without a chapter focusing on the world of business and the experience of leading large public institutions, and Rick Haythornthwaite has risen to the very top of both types of enterprise. He became the chairman of MasterCard in 2006 and held that role for fifteen years; he was the chairman of Centrica for five years between 2014 and 2019 and is currently the independent non-executive chairman of Ocado Group. From the late seventies until the mid-nineties, he was employed by the oil giant BP in various roles, including as the general manager of the Magnus oilfield, which is situated nearly one hundred miles north-east of the Shetland Islands in the North Sea. Being the chairman of MasterCard had its perks and one of those was having the best table at the BRIT Awards, the one closest to the stage, within touching distance of some of the world's biggest music stars, as MasterCard was the headline sponsor of the entire event. Rick would often invite my wife and me as his guests and it was here, away from the boardrooms that were his natural habitat, that I saw how adept he was at making anyone feel comfortable in his presence. Whether I introduced him to Ed Sheeran, Sam Fender or Stormzy, this distinguished Oxbridge-educated man in his sixties who stands at over six feet tall never patronised or looked uninterested in anyone who came to our table.

Assembling a group of strangers to spend an evening in each other's company is a work of art to behold and he was the Tate Modern and National Portrait Gallery combined when it came to curating a table of great conversationalists. Over those five years of attending the BRIT Awards, I sat next to the man who invented the internet, the first Black man to captain the England rugby team and a duke who likes to let people drive fast cars around his ancestral home. I have seen him conduct a symphonia of conversation and witnessed many times his ability to cut through the detritus of unnecessary debate and get to the point – this man is without question a professional conversationalist. This is why Rick was one of the very first people I interviewed for *Let's Talk*.

I started by asking him how he became so proficient at talking to people from such a vast array of backgrounds. Is it something that comes from simply having had very many conversations with different sorts of people or had he been sent somewhere to learn these skills? He told me that he had been sent to a management consultancy firm in the US to specifically learn about what having good conversations in business really meant, though he has, of course, had a lifetime of doing the former.

Rick began by outlining his philosophy for having meaningful conversations: 'If you are really going to engage with people, you've got to enter into their space and you've got to be who you need to be within that space. But there is a core of who you are that remains constant.' In the context of a conversation, what does this actually mean? By entering into 'their space', is there a need to adopt a role, to be malleable and chameleon-like? I wanted to dig a little deeper to discover more about what it takes to be able to make connections with individuals who have differing agendas and backgrounds. According to Rick, it's about developing the ability to adjust yourself to whatever the situation demands: 'The confidence comes from knowing who you are, but actually it's a carapace that can morph according to who's around, what the circumstances are and what you're trying to achieve.' As to whether it is down to nature or nurture, Rick simply says, 'It's a learned skill.' One that he has spent decades cultivating.

'The ability to engage with anyone, whether it was on an oil rig, or in a factory, or in the boardroom, is a necessary skill because, in the end, what you're trying to do is engage,' Rick explained. The word 'engagement' here is key to understanding the necessity of effective communication. To effectively articulate what it is you need someone else to achieve, and also accomplish what it is you need to do, requires thoughtful examination of the words you use. This can make the difference between successfully fulfilling those objectives and falling short. The earlier you find common ground with someone, the quicker you can get to the exciting part of exploring the possibilities that come with collaboration.

After decades of experience in both the private and public sectors, Rick still focuses on the power of words and how much preparation needs to go into having important conversations – 'I will still think it through and I will rehearse it quietly.' For much of this book, the emphasis has been on the importance of being able to talk to each other; what Rick adds to this is how well prepared we have to be in order to have certain types of conversations effectively.

My job involves a great deal of preparation. In fact, I approach every interview with an imaginary US football coach yelling in my ears: 'Fail to prepare, and prepare to fail!' This is not the same as rehearsing a script and then reciting it verbatim (which I don't do); it's about having the knowledge of the subject areas and the confidence that comes with having done your research. I have been in situations where people in leadership positions have used extraordinarily ineffectual and confidence-sapping words, which suggests a lack of thought and preparation. After all, with power comes responsibility – a well-worn phrase that some forget. Rick believes that, in business, your choice of words 'is very, very important, particularly the more senior you get; you owe it to people to be responsible for the words that come out of your mouth'. This wasn't always the case and he freely admits to having busked it in the early days of his career, but he soon learned that unless he was better prepared when entering into dialogues, they would just become 'a bland exchange of words'. For those in management, it is easy to become bogged down by the processes and, as career progression begets greater renumeration, to forget what is at the heart of being a good manager. For Rick, it was his boss at the time, who had recently returned from the prestigious American university Stanford, who told him to strip back the idea of management in order to 'think about who people are'.

Throughout *Let's Talk*, we return again and again to the connection that you must build with people in order to benefit from their thoughts and opinions, which in turn can help you to formulate new ideas and ways of seeing the world. As a much younger man, Rick was sent to an American consultancy firm called JMW specifically to learn how to have better conversations. They began by telling the assembled future leaders that they were never going to carry a hammer or a spanner as a job requirement, so the only tools they had at their disposal were the words that came out of their mouths. Away from the language of business, they had to 'get rid of all that bullshit that people create in the workplace', as Rick delicately puts it. Those in attendance were encouraged to read the works of the American philosopher Richard Rorty and those of the German philosopher Friedrich Nietzsche and to get know themselves, first, to look inwards and ask, 'What are you really committed to as an individual?' The nature of truth and the nature of commitment were at the heart of what the attendees were motivated to explore.

The course made Rick think about who he was, who he wanted to be and whether he needed to have two different personas, depending on whether he was at home or at work. The demands of the office setting mean we may purposefully create two separate characters: the person we want our colleagues to see and the one our family and friends experience away from our working environments. Perhaps the kind of workplace culture you find yourself a part of demands the kind of attitude that wouldn't work when asking your partner to put the bins out or making sure your kids have cleaned their bedrooms. If so, then is that the right place for you? After asking himself who he wanted to be in the office and if that should be a different person to who he was at home, Rick could see that his answer was a categorical 'no'. The same principles, morals and integrity he practised beyond the confines of a working environment had to exist fully within it.

Upon deciding to live by a set of principles that do not waver no matter the setting, it was then an imperative to bring that out in others. Rick described this as a 'conversation about discovery', the purpose being to ascertain what is important to that person sitting in front of you and use that knowledge to further the conversation. When two or more people are trying to discover something about each other, their words should be considered and used carefully. He asked, 'Is it about closure, is it about action, is it about breakdown? Every one of those conversations have different forms, they have different words, different verbs, and if you hold one conversation and you're trying to achieve another, you'll confuse the person on the other end.' Be certain going into the conversation what the objectives are and tailor the words used accordingly. When you are clear from the very beginning what is being attempted, crossed wires and unaligned goals can be avoided. This may seem obvious, but how often does confusion arise because two people have approached a dialogue from vastly different viewpoints, wasting a significant amount of time as a result. At the crux of the exercise was the commitment to 'holding high-quality conversations'. The quality element coming from the clarity of purpose. In board meetings at the Southbank Centre, Rick was always very clear about the issue at hand. There was no ambiguity regarding what needed to be discussed. This prevented the conversation from veering off into irrelevancy. It saved time and focused the mind.

At just forty-two, Rick became a CEO. Because of

what he had learned previously in the US about personal communication and how that applies to organisational structure, he knew that an organisation, in order to be successful, consisted of just ten conversations that really mattered. The discovery part was identifying what those ten were and then making sure that they were of the highest quality. It may seem like an oversimplification to limit yourself to so few conversations, but therein lies the challenge and the benefit. To avoid being bogged down by innumerable dialogues, focus on finding those ten that matter most.

Not being an entrepreneur myself, I wondered how much time CEOs and chairs have to be truly reflective and introspective in this way. After speaking to Rick, it seems vital to be able to look inwards, identify who you are and what your goals are, and then, from those jumping-off points of self-assuredness, begin the work of drawing people together through first-class dialogues. As we went deeper into this territory, I genuinely felt like I was in the presence of a guru of conversation. I had witnessed Rick chairing Southbank Centre board meetings with a calm authority. I had never seen him rattled, raise his voice or try to humiliate anyone. In a career that has spanned so many industries, roles and huge pressures, what were the most difficult conversations to have? 'The most difficult conversations are obviously the ones that involve people who are underperforming and are unlikely ever to perform at the level you need them to.' Not every dialogue leads to a positive outcome, especially where there is likely to be a parting of ways between employer and employee. Respect and clarity are needed in such a situation.

Another challenging area Rick identified is a CEO who is trying to encourage his employees to go beyond what they think is possible. This blockage in thinking occurs because, according to Rick, they 'can't see beyond the silo in which they currently exist and in which they've invested intensely'. The silo in question could be the role that they have either defined for themselves or one that has been foisted upon them by the organisation. To see what lies beyond that and be able to imagine it is what Rick wants to encourage. As a leader, your job is to get those people who are used to existing within the cosy confines of a silo to accept some risk; you want to expand and empower their imagination to believe that they have the agency to influence the system that they are working in.

So often when the excrement hits the fan or a complete 'balls-up', as Rick would say, occurs, people switch into panic mode, followed by blame distribution. In those challenging moments, it is difficult to see beyond the disaster that is unravelling before your very eyes. So if someone in a leadership position is unlucky enough to find themselves with a corporate calamity heading towards the bridge of their nose, then it would be wise to remember what Rick has learned in his long and successful career: 'I don't think that there is a single moment,' he said, 'that I have been through like that where we haven't come out better than when we entered the situation.' That is because rather than take a crisis straight to drama school, all of the sentiment connected to the problem is put to one side. 'The first key thing is to separate fact from emotion,' Rick explained. Acknowledge that the anger which is welling up inside of you is a completely natural phenomenon which makes you human, but that it is an energy that will not help anyone. 'Now get all that energy and commit it to finding the facts. Just being that person in that situation is transformational for everyone around you.' As Rudyard Kipling wrote at the end of the nineteenth century: 'If you can keep your head when all about you are losing theirs . . .' In the twenty-first century, those words still ring true. And, as Rick has been reminded many times in his career, the quality of the proceeding conversations will define how well the organisation emerges from a predicament. 'All of this is so important because, quite often, organisations are defined by their response to failure. The key to getting to the other side is holding the right conversation.' And it has to be one unfettered by emotions. This conviction that experiencing a crisis can ultimately strengthen an organisation may explain why Rick made a point of saying to me that he is 'an unreformed optimist' who is 'on a constant hunt for a silver lining'.

Rick places his almost Zen-like unflappability at the doors of a childhood experience that reinforced his ability to remain calm when people around him are 'going apoplectic'. Rick lost his mother at the age of eleven and he asks rhetorically, 'What worse thing can happen?' In order to approach problems in the way he does, we will have to effectively rewire ourselves to be able to acknowledge the emotions that get in the way of us having constructive conversations and 'basically putting a blocker in there', as he puts it.

As he has spent much time studying, refining and practising what he was taught about conversations, I asked Rick about the stages that a boss and a colleague will go through to get to a point where both parties are more than merely satisfied but feel that real progress can be made in both personal and professional development. Rick started his answer by taking a holistic look at how we see groupings of people: 'The first thing to recognise is that any organisation, society, tribe is basically a network of conversations.' People who are given leadership roles face many new responsibilities, not least of which is the power to help the people under their charge fully realise and fulfil their career aspirations. The way Rick breaks this down is fascinating. Firstly, it is about possibilities. If, as you look to your future, the view is blighted by the failure to see the possibilities, then your actions will reflect that lack of vision. Rick believes that enabling someone to see the potential before them is transformative. In a conversation with someone, he is 'always quietly trying to find out what do they see as possible in life, because when they see that something is possible, there's a natural excitement in what they're doing'. Allowing that person to verbalise what their dreams and aspirations are releases an energy into the exchange and that reimagining is an expansion of the mind.

Once that broadening of the imagination takes place,

then the next stage necessitates action. Stage two involves discovering what practical steps are needed in order for the imagination and the application of it to converge. As part of the transition from stage one to stage two, it's important to start to use words associated with action, so those possibilities can be realised and do not remain caged by a lack of confidence. From initially investigating the possibilities to then defining the actions needed, the discourse then evolves into one about 'accountability and commitment'. But Rick was keen to add an important note of caution to this seemingly linear progression. It is vital that as a figure of authority in the business you do not box the person in. You have to give them the permission to say no, otherwise they may overpromise and under-deliver. 'Too often,' Rick said, 'people are saying, "OK, can you do this by next week? Great thanks." As opposed to, "Let's have a negotiation and find a commitment that you now feel responsible for."' The art of persuasion can be employed to trick us into thinking that we have made the decision, when, in fact, we have been manipulated into acting in a way that most benefits the person we are talking to. This book is about trying to discover the art of conversation, rather than persuasion, so Rick's policy of achieving shared goals through consensus is both sensible and ultimately more rewarding for both parties.

Rick went on to describe to me a beautiful life hack that I am so far from achieving, but it does provide something I want to work towards. As his day begins to come to an end and if he is feeling 'unsettled', Rick makes a conscious effort to go back through his day and ask himself the question 'What didn't I close out?' This idea of closing out the day is important. But it isn't defined as an unsent email or an overlooked piece of admin. It is more personal and human than that. His words strike a chord with me, mostly because I leave so many things unfinished and delay dealing with them because they feel overwhelming. But Rick doesn't do procrastination: 'I can always find something that I didn't do and I will complete it. I'll pick up the phone to [a team member] and say, "I should've said this earlier that you've done a great job." By closing out, I'm opening out to thinking again.' How can something be so revelatory and common-sense in equal measure? The profundity isn't in the logic of ending the day with an empty out-tray but in the freedom it gives you the following morning because you will not be dragged down by the accumulating demands of unfinished business.

As a person progresses up the career ladder and finds themselves in the highest echelons of corporate power, how do they act as the grandiosity of the job titles, the salaries and the egos grow exponentially? Walking into a room full of alphas who are used to having people hang on their every word cannot make for an environment where witty exchanges, empathetic dialogue and curiosity thrives. Especially in a boardroom. Knowing full well that Rick is not one of those types, I was intrigued to learn how he deals with that kind of person in a corporate setting. How do you manage an individual who loves the sound of their own voice so much that if they were made of ice cream they would lick themselves into oblivion? 'You signal the most important ground rule by not speaking first. You make it clear that we are just going to have a conversation for a while and I want to hear all opinions.' From the outset, the de facto leader in the room is declaring that he/she is there to listen and not begin proceedings by telling everyone what his or her own views are and potentially stifling a discussion before it has even begun. This gives those present the licence to express their opinions without fear or favour. This immediately creates a flat hierarchy in the room, as opposed to a vertical one. All views are given equal validity. It is also important to not allow any one person to dominate the proceedings. By bringing this clarity into the room, Rick is immediately ensuring that there is no need to embarrass someone further down the line for allowing their ego to override the ground rules. It works because, as a trustee sitting in that room, there is the tacit understanding that all opinions are valid and equitable and that a reasonable amount of time and space will be given over to ensure that every trustee feels listened to. It is obvious that such an approach should not be confined to chairing a board meeting of a globally recognised artistic organisation.

Rick is a physically imposing man with an intimidating CV who wields great power in the organisations he leads. In that context, how does he ensure that those who wish to speak to him do not feel intimidated or overawed? 'I try to be approachable. Be interested. Don't be pompous. You need to show them pretty rapidly that there is nothing to be afraid of here.' He is always well versed in his brief, asks the most incisive questions and allows conversations to flow like a football referee who plays the advantage rather than stops the action for every minor misdemeanour.

With foresight, planning and a genuine curiosity, you can get the best from a conversation at work, but life doesn't always present us with interactions that can be planned for in advance. In both our business and private lives, there will be times where we are introduced to someone who we have never met before or placed in a situation that amplifies our sense that we are an impostor who is about to be exposed. If you are not brimming with confidence to begin with, then this type of scenario may feel like an ordeal. So what can you do in a situation such as this, when no preparation is possible and insecurities bubble up to the surface? Rick's advice was characteristically calming: 'One: relax. Two: they're not judging you. Everyone thinks they're being judged in the conversation. Actually, most people just want to have a conversation and if you can find, through questioning, that little point of connection, then you can just go from there.' He also revealed the perfect ice-breaker question if you find yourself sat next to a total stranger: 'What is it that you would love to be doing right now rather than speaking to me?' As long as the answer isn't 'Almost anything else in the world!' then you can imagine the tension just slipping away.

Communicating effectively with a wide range of people

who may have different goals and interests is an important skill and part of what makes Rick so successful. Before I interviewed him for this book, I had no idea that this skill was something that he had in fact been taught, at least in part. I had assumed that it was a natural outcome of a combination of genetics, his public school and Oxbridge education, and the confidence that naturally comes with attending such institutions. But, of course, the art of good conversation is in fact a craft, and one that can be practised and honed, with no trip to business school necessary. When you see a true master of verbal communication, remember that these are learned behaviours, not something innate which you are either born with or not. Which means not only can we become more effective communicators if we choose but that we should not let those who do not employ them off the hook when there is a better alternative.

Rick has had a career not without controversy, as you would expect from anyone who has worked in the energy sector and risen to his position of seniority. In all of my social and professional dealings with him, he has been both insightful and inspiring. What I have heard said about him when he is not in the room, which is always the best barometer of how the world sees an individual, mirrors my own experiences of being in his company.

As our chat neared its end, Rick wanted me to understand that there are two types of conversation that we have to be aware of – in life in general and not just in the boardroom. Type one 'is the mind throwing up its instinct, its gut feeling, etc., which has its place'. This can broadly be defined as an exchange of words driven by emotion. Utterances are shaped not by objectivity but by an impetuosity, which, in the wrong context, could make a bad situation even worse. A type two conversation, however, is 'the considered view when the mind is thinking' and is more measured in nature. The next time you approach a potentially sensitive conversation, ask yourself whether what you are about to say should be a type one utterance or a type two sequence of thoughts verbalised. I think we both know which would usually be the preferred option, but our minds do not work from pre-programmed algorithms. As Rick acknowledges, there is a time and a place for a type one conversation, but when important dialogues have to take place, your default setting should be type two and we know why. In circumstances that are difficult or tense, the type two conversationalist will achieve far more than the type one version.

Rick explained one of the inherent problems of working with a group of non-executive board members who turn up just seven times a year: 'We put multibillion-dollar decisions in front of them and give them a fifteen-minute presentation and five minutes to make their minds up, it's bullshit.' To mitigate against this imperfect scenario and help the board to make better, more considered decisions, Rick ensures no room is left for the executives to use emotions and instincts to dictate the direction of travel. Instead, he said, 'I will make sure they basically have a discovery, exploration and decision. Three bites of the cherry, so forcing them into type two thinking as opposed to letting them get away with the far more enjoyable but rather random type one thinking.' He puts the brakes on any inclination to be impetuous and, in so doing, enables everybody to make more informed choices which form the bedrock of type two thinking.

One of the things that most impresses me about Rick is his seemingly unquenchable curiosity. His probing intellect never seems to take time off, driven as it is by a relentless optimism. Not many of us have the resources that he has at his disposal, nor the connections that he has spent years acquiring, but we do have the capability to be inquisitive. It is paramount that we understand the usefulness of this if we are to constantly refine how we conduct the conversations in our lives. The tutoring Rick received all those years ago sparked in him an inquisitiveness that age has not watered down. Even now, he said, he is 'on permanent inquiry about how to hold more effective conversations'. His professional success has placed him in a position to constantly use and refine these skills: 'That's why becoming a chairman has been so great, because my whole life is orchestrating conversations. That's all I do.' All of his leadership dealings are unambiguously 'about making sure that the right people get together and hold high-quality conversations about the right topics and come to conclusions when they need to come to conclusions'.

The energy that comes from good interactions powers so many of the decisions that we make. Please think about the exchanges that you have at work and then ask yourself if they are being led by someone who is genuinely trying to discover what the purpose of a good conversation is. Is this person allowing those in the room to realise their own promise? Are they empowering them to believe that they can influence the system that they are working within and expand their own idea of what is possible? This goes way beyond the desire for a short-term promotion and into the realm of what they dream about for themselves. The unlocking of ambition, the opening of a door that had once seemed closed and the revelation that a person is capable of so much more than they think they are can all be achieved by an insightful conversation.

The more I think about what Rick said, the less sure I am that many people in leadership positions really under-stand how to have these valuable dialogues. Stripping away the debris of negativity that blocks our ability to recognise our own talents and opening ourselves up to consider what new futures await us sounds like the kind of management speak that you would probably avoid if someone other than me were telling you about it. It is easy to be cynical about such instructions because they take no note of the petty-minded office politicking that can sometimes take place, which sees people ill-qualified to turn a tap on having authority bestowed upon them. The tendency to overcomplicate a situation is often born of a realisation that someone is out of their depth. In order to compensate for a lack of confidence, they use words to dig themselves out of a hole, while simultaneously sinking even further.

While I cannot guarantee that the cream will always rise to the top in any organisation, I do believe that the future of work will see a greater churn of workers as younger generations have no grasp of what a job for life would look like and perhaps wouldn't want one even if it were offered to them. In a competitive job market where a multitude of positions remain unfilled and companies are battling it out to hire the best talent, other than pay, what inducements will lure the brightest and the best into the corporate fold? People often talk about the culture of an organisation in both derogatory and glowing terms. Different workplaces have different cultures, some that are inclusive and supportive and others that are divisive and toxic. To go back to Rick's point, if businesses want to prove that theirs is a place that will be financially and holistically rewarding, they will have to commit to having conversations internally that are of a similar quality to the ones they aspire to have externally.

12

Matthew Syed:
Hierarchies in Business

Every time Matthew Syed has appeared on my radio show, the reaction from the audience has been astonishing. Across all social media and the texts and WhatsApp messages I receive, I can see immediately that people are fascinated by his take on the world. His ability to be able to counteract the irrational with common sense, communicate complicated ideas in a palatable way and inspire the mind to think differently is almost beyond compare. He has written six bestselling books, including *Bounce*, *Black Box Thinking* and the simply brilliant *Rebel Ideas*. As a result of his insightful and incisive work in the fields of mindset growth, leadership and high performance, he has had the opportunity on many occasions to speak to world-leading organisations about the dangers of entrenched thinking, untapped potential in workforces and the importance of diversity – where the word diversity means much more than the colour of someone's skin.

When I first read *Rebel Ideas*, which encourages us all to embrace different viewpoints and escape the echo chambers, the clarity of the propositions contained within the book gave me ample food for thought. His attacks on the culture of groupthink, the paucity of imagination in large companies and the failure to recognise the benefits of a diverse workforce were as prescient as they were self-evident.

I began our conversation by asking Matthew how much value he felt businesses place on the ability of their people to have good conversations. After a moment's thought, he said, 'I think that people take this too much for granted.' Part of the problem is the traditional structure of businesses. With most business entities being largely hierarchical in nature, it is inevitable that the authority figures at the top exhibit a certain inability to recognise and accept the advice of subordinates. They 'do a lot of the talking and not enough of the listening,' according to Matthew, 'so the information tends to flow downwards from the top.' While he accepts that that is vital in certain circumstances, he explained that there is not enough knowledge travelling in the opposite direction. He believes that by ignoring this invaluable source of ideas, simply because they lack seniority, a company is missing out on vital insights. He is adamant that within companies 'more should be done to facilitate strong, meaningful, authentic, trusting conversations', while at the same time acknowledging that 'it's a difficult thing to do'.

So what then does a master communicator such as

Matthew Syed define as a strong, meaningful, authentic and trusting connection? Does he also believe that the skill of communicating with others is a talent that can be pursued, nurtured and enhanced? In answer to my first question, I fully expected Matthew to describe in technical detail what his definition of a conversationalist was, employing the terminology of business and the experience of countless days spent illuminating the minds of CEOs. I was poised to transcribe an academic's definition laid out in cold prose. What I got instead was a very personal recollection of someone who clearly made a big impression on Matthew's life.

'When you use that term [conversationalist], I think of my grandfather on my mother's side.' Matthew described him as a man who 'had an amazing ability to draw people out of themselves'. His mother's father was also a great storyteller, which, of course, tends to involve quite considerable oratorical expertise. What set his grandfather apart as a real master of conversation was that even though he could quite easily have directed all of the focus in the room towards himself, 'he made sure he didn't dominate any given conversation.'

As he ran through a list of his grandfather's personality traits, I could not help thinking that what Matthew was also doing was describing how to be a good person and it was clear that Matthew was still in awe of this remarkable man. 'He always used to ask somebody an open question and if they only said "yes" or "no", he would use his hand as if to say "come on, let us hear a bit more about it".'

As well as inviting people to open up, Matthew explained that his grandfather also noticed those on the periphery of the group and ensured they were invited in and that their contribution was welcomed.

It seems evident that Matthew's grandfather wanted to connect those in the room to each other through dialogue and that he was cognisant of the gains to be had by being self-aware in a social setting: avoiding dominating the room, eliciting openness and inviting others to contribute. Taking this as a model, look at the people around you in the room as if they are the brass, woodwind, percussion and strings of an orchestra. Imagine then your role as the conductor making sure that everyone has a chance to play their part, which combines to create a fluidity of sound. This is what Matthew was describing as he warmly re-called how his grandfather empowered the people around him and never took over a conversation or a room.

To give an example of the capacity of people to learn these skills, Matthew talked about his own shortcomings in the sphere of public speaking. For him, this is still a conversation, but one that many people are listening to simultaneously. Standing up on a stage and addressing a room full of strangers is a very common fear, besides the obvious ones of a giant meteorite hitting the Earth, spiders and clowns. Shortly after his book *Bounce* was published, Matthew was invited to speak at a globally renowned investment bank. The institution in question has a reputation for hiring the most ambitious, academi-cally gifted and tenacious candidates available. Here was a man transitioning from being a table tennis player to an author, so he wasn't exactly pumped up on self-confidence as he mounted the stage to address this gathering of multi-billion-pound deal-making alphas. Nor had he done much public speaking at this point, which only exacerbated his feelings of impostor syndrome. All of his nightmares were realised as his proclamations were polluted by a lack of authority, he was heckled a few times and his anxiety levels began to develop an inverse relationship with his confidence.

After finishing the speech, he vowed never to attempt public speaking again. He conjured up a list of reasons why the stage was no longer for him: he didn't have 'the natural eloquence or the social confidence to command the stage', he told himself, and he found it 'difficult to read the room' because he is by nature quite an anxious individual. If you were being honest right now, how many of those labels would you attribute to yourself?

However, what eventually became obvious to Matthew following the debacle at the investment bank was that by accepting his own shortcomings as intractable, he was effectively 'shutting off' his future development. As a former Olympian who had spent years working towards a set goal, this was a situation he could not readily embrace. He decided to contact a company that specialised in giving people the 'social confidence' to speak in public. Over the course of three years, Matthew attended meetings every two weeks. Over time, he became more adept at communicating to groups of people. One of the exercises he did in the group sessions involved going to the front of the room and flipping over a card, revealing a topic to be spoken about for one minute in front of the fifteen other people in the meeting. Each person was then encouraged to make their way to the front and critique each other's speeches. The purpose of this and other scenarios of this kind was to give every individual present a chance to speak to the whole. What Matthew's single-mindedness in addressing what he saw as a shortcoming proves is that what you think you lack in conversational skills can be improved upon over time – or, as Matthew put it, 'they're buildable'.

In his experience, the three elements needed to overcome self-doubt and evolve are: 'a mindset where you're seeking to learn, decent mentoring and not giving up the first time you hit an obstacle'. These are, of course, life lessons which are applicable to a myriad of different challenges that you may face, not exclusively suited to the development of conversational skills, but if you doubt whether you can ever become someone who holds a meeting in the palm of your hand or manages to draw out significant aspects of who someone is in the course of a dialogue, then remember where the now constantly in-demand public speaker, author and journalist Matthew Syed began. To give you some idea of how successfully he has overcome his initial misgivings, he now does between 100 and 150 such talks every year.

There is a danger, though, of developing a monolithic structure that encases your own truths within it if you are constantly relied upon to provide words of wisdom to rooms full of people nodding compliantly. How does someone in this position prevent themselves from starting to assume that their opinions are unassailable facts? Matthew's view is that inhabiting an echo chamber is a 'catastrophe' and the way to avoid that is by employing some humility and accepting fully that 'you don't have a monopoly on truth'. This principle is so important if we are to have better conversations with each other. Steadfastly sticking to a narrow position and refusing to recognise the views of others is where so many individuals, media outlets and social media algorithms have been herding us and Matthew is all too aware of that. He noted that 'a certain level of arrogance has started to infiltrate these echo chambers where people in particular ideological niches think they have a monopoly on truth'.

For anyone who has spent even a few minutes on social media in the last six months trying to assess the political landscape, that is a sentence that will ring true. When we talk about 'filter bubbles' and 'echo chambers', we are potentially denying that we exist in them too. When we have challenging conversations with those we perceive are inside them, the temptation is to believe it is them who need to change their views or broaden their outlook, instead of conducting a closer inspection and interrogation of our own. If a conversation, particularly one fraught with potential pitfalls due to political differences, is entered into with the purpose of changing the other person's views to align with your own, then studies suggest that it may end up having the opposite effect.

Research first published in 2020 but based on data collected during the 2016 presidential race, one of the most divisive elections in US history, suggests that by simply asking someone to leave their 'filter bubble', you may in fact persuade them to stay even more encased in it. This is because the natural reaction to a challenging dialogue is not to seek out opinions that are counter to your own but to look for more evidence to confirm those already held. Put into an American context, the research suggests that when a liberal challenges a conservative, there is no attempt by that conservative to build a bridge by exploring views counter to their own. Rather than automatically switching from Fox News to CNN, for example, the conservative will delve deeper into right-wing news outlets that corroborate already firmly held orthodoxies. In addition, liberals who spoke to other liberals would tend to increase their use of liberal media outlets and move even further away from right-leaning news programming as their trust of them ebbed away. Classifying yourself as a liberal and largely conversing with other liberals will mainly result in you burrowing yourself deeper and deeper into a media echo chamber that challenges none of your beliefs either. You will have to proactively seek out contrasting views in order to establish a broader set of facts rather than cherry-picking those that substantiate your own opinions.

Allow me to cite an example from my own adventures in the Twittersphere. After I suggested that there may be parallels between the language used by Trump supporters towards supporters of Joe Biden after his 2020 US election victory and the words used by Remain supporters to describe those who voted Leave in the 2016 EU Referendum, all hell broke loose. The ensuing pile-on was something to behold. Certain Remain voters, unequivocal in the belief of their own moral superiority, were aghast that their denial of the legitimacy of the result and questioning of the intelligence of those who voted Leave could in any way be compared to how the Trump faithful talked about the US election result and those who voted in opposition to how they did.

From the pitfalls of the online and political echo chambers, let's return to the subject of businesses and specifically those individuals who sit at the top of the corporate tree, 'where,' Matthew said, 'you can have a leadership that thinks they know everything'. He paraphrased the CEO of Microsoft, Satya Nadella, who, upon taking over at the giant tech company in 2014, signalled a change in culture from that of a 'know it all' outlook to that of a 'learn it all' one. Those who believe they know it all tend to talk incessantly; we have all met them and they are, at best, boring and, at worst, narcissistic bullies. Migrating from that standpoint to one which recognises the need to listen more than to talk is a recurring theme throughout this book, one which we cannot overstate the importance of.

I asked Matthew to tell me about the last great conversation he had had, and what made it so. I was expecting him to wax lyrical about a particularly impressive CEO that he had recently dined with, but his inspiration came from much closer to home. 'It's not difficult to explain this one because I spent Saturday and Sunday with my nine-year-old daughter.' That all-too-precious daddy-and-daughter time clearly made an impression on him. 'It was just beautiful sitting down and talking to her about life, how she feels about the world, how she feels about me as a dad, about her school, about friendship, about society.' This connection spurred Matthew into telling me about a strategy he employs when in a room of people. If harvesting different perspectives is something you aspire to, then it would be useful to employ Matthew's rule: 'I try to talk to the oldest and the youngest in the group.' By focusing on these two individuals in the room, Matthew is much more likely to hear two different perspectives and, through that, potentially reshape his own perspective on the world.

I hope this part of the book has demonstrated that learning to have better conversations is a tangible and achievable goal to set for yourself. As with going to the gym or eating a healthier diet, the activity of studying how you listen and talk to others should be a regular practice and an integral part of how you see yourself growing and flourishing in the future.

Not everyone is either willing to be, or capable of being, a leader. Whether you seek greatness or have greatness thrust upon you, be mindful of how you use that power and the accompanying responsibility. Leadership takes many forms, whether it be as a parent, guardian or carer, a mentor or a manager with a small team. What I learned from interviewing both Rick and Matthew is that leadership is all about challenging preconceptions, effective communication and humility; the understanding of how to speak to people and what to say but also being humble enough to know that you do not have all of the answers. If you cannot form your ideas through collaboration, which is fed by an ability to listen to others, then how good a leader can you really be? The ideas that both men have shared are not born of magical powers that only they possess. Through decades of experience, observation and an insatiable curiosity, they have forged incredibly successful careers. You may not be a CEO, chair or board member, or be invited in to companies to address their senior leadership teams, but you may find yourself in a situation that requires a calm, dispassionate response. In which case, I hope that you can lean on the words of both of my interviewees in order to be able to navigate the right path through difficult times. To do this, you must be able to recognise the power of a high-quality conversation.

PART 5

THE PROFESSIONAL CONVERSATIONALIST

13

Let's Talk About Interviews

I now work almost exclusively in the field of speech radio, as opposed to a DJ who talks between songs, and it is a ravenous beast that requires feeding twenty-four hours a day. It gorges on information, which places teams of producers and broadcast journalists in the unenviable position of having to make sure the beast is not left wanting. The people who work in this particular realm of radio, presenters included, are on the constant hunt for morsel after morsel of ear-grabbing news. It is largely reactive as breaking stories are processed and converted into chunks of digestible information. Roving journalists seek out localised leads or are sent to cover stories that occur on their patch. Experts are plucked out of an address book and thrown into the limelight to provide (hopefully) comprehensively pithy analyses of ongoing crises. Legions of publicists send through press releases about a new book, album, TV show or revolutionary beard trimmer and pray for a bit of positive publicity. People are tasked with trawling through the myriad of opinions expressed by texters, emailers, tweeters, Facebook posters and WhatsAppers, which range from the lucid and profound to the terminally misinformed. Once all of these information feeds are collated, truncated and have been through the editorial filter, my job is to link all of the constituent parts together and keep your attention fixed on me for as long as possible. When the red light comes on in my studio, indicating that the mic is 'live', from this point on, the nation can hear every word that I say. I am ready to build a one-on-one conversation with my audience. This is what makes me a professional conversationalist.

The job does not require me to sit there and stitch together a sequence of soliloquies for the betterment of my listeners. I am only ever in 'project and connect mode', which aims to make sure what I am saying is relatable and digestible. Unlike television and film, which by their very nature needs far more time to develop and execute an idea, the medium of communication where I ply my trade is immediate and relentless in its need to make sure that the audiences are constantly informed and entertained. It is live, intimate and participatory in a way that no other form of entertainment really is. For me, that is the true magic of radio. Documentary film-makers generally have access to teams who can spend months and even years chasing down leads, entering and getting out of creative cul-de-sacs and piecing together a complicated narrative. In radio, the churn of constantly trying to fill an empty space hour after hour, day after day, does not allow us the luxury of time. It also means that on occasion we feel the frustration that we may not have done a subject the justice it deserves. Seven minutes on the turmoil in Afghanistan followed by six minutes on a natural disaster affecting thousands of lives doesn't seem enough, but sometimes it has to be.

Then there is always the chance that a speech broadcaster could be presented with an idea or news story just hours or even minutes before they go on air, having to conduct a two- or three-way conversation about it for an entire hour with little notice. On these occasions, I rely on a relentlessly curious and industrious team to work with me to secure the right guests and prepare detailed briefs that are free of mistakes.

As part of this journalistic work, we must always be thinking about how we are framing the conversation for our audience. We want to avoid a listener feeling that we have taken a superficial approach to an issue that requires thought, care and due diligence. We have to also be vigilant to not make crass gear changes in subject matter that leave the listener feeling uncomfortable. As a broadcaster, the last thing you want to do is switch from a story about abuse, trauma or death to one about a man who found a carrot on his allotment that resembles Daniel Craig's face. So making sure that the different elements that go into the show can remain eclectic without being jarring is important.

One of the greatest compliments that any broadcaster

can receive is when someone messages to say that at the beginning of an interview, they thought that they would have no interest in the interviewee or the subject matter, but after just a few minutes they were hooked. That is the power of a great conversation: even if you are not a direct participant, you are drawn into it. The three hours a day that I spend broadcasting to the nation allow me to do what I do best, which is have deeper and longer conversations. My show has been gifted the freedom to explore different experiences of a life in greater detail and the latitude to ask that follow-up question knowing that the confines of time aren't demanding a sound bite instead of an in-depth response. These long-form interviews give space for a meaningful connection to exist between interviewer, interviewee and listener.

Most of the well-known guests are booked weeks in advance, which means that each day is usually quite comprehensively mapped out. Unless a guest drops out at the last minute, which happens fairly regularly, and then the team is tasked with filling that time slot with a guest or topic and I have to be across the subject matter pronto. There are, though, the odd unique occasions whereby a breaking news story instantly erases everything that had been planned for the show.

On Wednesday 22 March 2017 at 2.40 p.m., a terrorist mounted the pavement and drove through crowds of people on Westminster Bridge. Fifty people were injured, of which thirty-one needed hospital treatment, and five people very sadly were killed. As I sat in my studio near

Manchester that afternoon, every script that had been written for a normal show on a normal day suddenly became irrelevant. As a clearer picture of what was taking place 200 miles away from where we were took shape, my role was to make sure that the listeners were kept constantly updated with eyewitness reports and official updates, and to string together the various strands of a constantly moving series of events.

I distinctly remember speaking to a newspaper journalist whose offices overlooked the spot at which the terrorist was shot dead by an armed police officer. From his vantage point, he could see the terrorist lying on the floor surrounded by armed police officers. The outline of guests then began to appear in the show's running order. The production team connected me to an MP who was locked inside the House of Commons along with a party of schoolchildren who had been touring the building.

In the midst of the uncertainty, the anguish of those in the area and the speed at which these terrible events were unfolding, my job was to calmly report on what we knew, avoid unsubstantiated testimony and, most importantly, ensure that the tone was neither voyeuristic nor sensationalist. Circumstances such as these require an entirely different type of broadcasting. Simplicity is key. During events as traumatic as these, clearly defined questions are required, especially because the person speaking isn't re-living terrible incidents that occurred in their past but is describing what is happening at that moment, with all the confusion and fear that that entails. There were hundreds if not thousands of people across news organisations that day who did their very best to make sure that the country, and indeed the entire world, could get a sense of what was unravelling on Westminster Bridge.

The events on that terrible day and the style of broadcasting that was required were anomalous when compared to what my show usually sounds like, which is three hours spent interviewing big guests from the worlds of music, TV, literature, theatre, film, philosophy and science. In those twelve hours, listeners are invited to join me in exploring other people's lives. I conduct conversations that require patience and focus, but also emotional investment. All the qualities that a genuine moment of human interaction needs. The show is focused on having exchange after exchange with people from across the societal, racial, sexual and political spectrum, which I do, not as a reporter linking once piece of pre-recorded audio to another but as a curious individual who wants to explore the multifaceted stories of my fellow human beings.

The stories we cover come from a wide variety of different places, but the promotion of a memoir is the motivation for many of the big guests who appear on my show. This reaches fever pitch during the months of September through until late November, when the leading book publishers are releasing what they hope will be their final-quarter money-spinners. In these months, I am inundated with material to read from actors, sportsmen and women, musicians and others in the public eye who have decided, or been persuaded, to bare all. These are some of the most revealing discussions, because what is usually out of bounds becomes an integral part of the chat. A publicist can request, or order, a production team not to talk about a film star's family history if they are there to promote a movie or TV show. These parameters disappear once said star has devoted 300 pages plus to dissecting who they are and where they came from. The invitation to pry has then been gifted to me on a silver platter.

During these months, I may be handed three or four books a week from my production team and while they very kindly offer to summarise the books for me and write a set of questions, I quite often decline the offer. Experience has taught me that developing my own line of questioning often uncovers the unnoticed parts of a biography and leads to a much more unique interaction with the guest. This is why I will never read out questions that were written for me. My producers, the book publishers and the authors expect, quite reasonably, that when the time comes and the microphones are faded up, I have grasped the text to such an extent that I can sustain a lengthy and in-depth conversation that will keep my audience's attention served. When you are sat in front of the philosopher A. C. Grayling, the theoretical physicist Carlo Rovelli, CNN's Chief International Correspondent Clarissa Ward or the rock star Chrissie Hynde (not all at the same time), you had better be on top of the brief. If you have failed to prepare, you will find yourself drowning in a sea of your own ineptitude, and they will sense that. The preparation that an interviewer puts into an interview shows how much they respect their guest and how seriously they take their job. These are people who are at the zenith of their chosen craft and it would be discourteous to them and disregarding of their achievements to treat them as a means of simply filling up airtime.

It would, of course, be vulgar to cite the amount of times a guest has commented on how much they have enjoyed our encounter. But as I am not above a bit of vulgarity, the rock star Sir Rod Stewart said to me at the end of our thirty minutes together, 'I've got to tell you, this is one of the best interviews I've done. That was really probing and just gorgeous. Thank you. You'd done your homework.' After interviewing comedian, actor and screenwriter Ricky Gervais in April 2020, he posted on Twitter: 'I'd like to say what a great broadcaster Nihal is. Well on his way to becoming a national treasure. Informed, open-minded, fair, astute, caring and funny. A dying breed.' Probably best that I stop now before I have an immodestygasm. Perhaps I need to remind myself of a quote by the maverick Italian footballer Mario Balotelli, who is reported to have once replied when asked why he didn't celebrate after scoring a goal, 'I don't celebrate because I am only doing my job. When a postman delivers letters, does he celebrate?' I have a genuine interest and respect for what these people do but also who they are. So it feels like the very least I can do is be fully invested in the guest and their story, and make sure that we both enjoy the experience and, most importantly, that the audience does too.

There is, of course, no guarantee of the degree of connection I will manage to achieve with my guest or how far they will open up. Not every single conversation will be so engrossing that a listener is unable to leave their car as they sit transfixed. That is always the aim, though. This is the world of the professional conversationalist, where what is being said matters, should be listened to and given space to be reacted to. From Guy Garvey, the frontman of the band Elbow, to the most famous boxing promoter on planet Earth Eddie Hearn, so many of my interviewees have finished our conversation saying that it felt more like a counselling session than a straightforward promotional opportunity. This is not because I am a trained counsellor but because I think, I listen and I react. As opposed to the five- or seven-minute slot mostly given over to a big guest interview on radio, I have twenty-five to fifty minutes to talk to a person of interest. This means that we can have a proper sit-down chat. That amount of time with an interesting person requires more research and more thought than the customary time limit slotted into a show's running order, where three or four questions should suffice and then on to the next one.

Meeting incredibly famous people is something that I am very much used to now, but there are those who still make me feel nervous. Week after week, I am presented with a plethora of stars who have been interviewed hundreds of times and have learned the craft of being professionally nice but who also, I suspect, yearn to be asked more searching questions than they are used to. When listening to a conversation between an interviewer and interviewee, try to notice who you hear most of during the exchanges. If the guest isn't doing the majority of the talking, then the interviewer has failed miserably. At the end of a long day spent fulfilling promotional obligations, simply switching on the publicity autopilot button to answer the same questions cannot be a fulfilling experience.

Sometimes the artist in question is reticent to give interviews in the first place, believing that the work should speak for itself and that they are under no obligation to explain the inner workings of their creative mind to a stranger. These occasions are rare, but once a broadcaster can sense an interview is about to unravel, the key is to understand why that is, to be persistently engaged and to make sure they switch it up, not switch off. This is where a lack of planning can turn an interview from awkward to terminal. When reading their memoir or scouring the internet for long-forgotten things they have said, the purpose is not to try to dazzle the interviewee with never-before-asked questions.

When I spoke with the sporting impresario, and the most recognisable boxing promoter in the world, Eddie Hearn, the obvious line of questioning to begin with would be the world of heavyweight boxing and the names Anthony Joshua and Tyson Fury. After watching numerous videos of Eddie having to placate an irate boxer, or a rival promoter, I began to think about how intimidating that world was and what the rules were for surviving within it. So I started by asking Eddie what his dad, the famous sporting promoter Barry Hearn, had taught his son about dealing with people who would try to 'take liberties' with him. Essentially, those who would disrespect Eddie by attempting to act improperly, break their word or exploit what they believed to be his naivety. Historically, the sport of boxing has been linked to organised crime, violence outside of the ring and the preponderance of unsavoury characters at every level of the sport, so it was not an unreasonable question to ask. In that world, there must be an army of potential 'liberty takers'. Eddie chuckled to himself and said, 'That's a question I've never been asked, Nihal, but it's actually rule number one.' At that point, I knew that it was going to be a great conversation. Rather than focusing on what he had done, I wanted to know how he had become the man that he was, stepping out from his father's long and super successful shadow and building an empire of his own.

The key to being a professional conversationalist in my line of work is to think about the human questions over the headline-grabbing ones, but also to have the courage to ask the questions that you would think about asking but feel nervous to actually ask. If a friend or relative said something that you found offensive, your instinct may be to move on from the comment immediately rather than questioning where the sentiment came from. If there has been a bereavement, you may find it easier to avoid the subject rather than meet it head on. These questions must, of course, be asked with tact and sensitivity, but to ignore them altogether does everyone involved a disservice.

These dialogues are also about having the mental agility to be able to react instantly as the situation changes. When the living legend that is Sir Paul McCartney sat down in front of me in December 2019, my immediate reaction was 'f*ck me, it's Paul McCartney', which isn't a very professional response or enlightening thought, and luckily I don't verbalise everything I'm thinking. I took that internal response to seeing this megastar for the first time and converted it into my very first question, jettisoning whatever one I had initially thought would kick-start our chat for the Penguin Podcast. I asked him, 'Do you feel that you always have to put people at ease because people are so nervous when they meet you?' His response was so modest and endearing. In that calming Liverpudlian drawl of his, he admitted to it being the case, but qualified it with something more fundamental about where he came from: 'A little bit, yeah, you do, but I think that's not just being famous, I think that's also Liverpool. It's a very Liverpool thing.' That initial question led quite naturally into one about who he would be nervous to talk to and this giant of popular culture admitted that he had once felt nervous about meeting Bob Dylan. When he eventually did at the US rock festival Coachella, or 'Oldchella' as he called it, since he was on the bill alongside such ageing luminaries of music as Neil Young and Dylan, he found the Nobel Prize-winning folk hero to be very nice. As I sat there in this tiny, nondescript room, in front of one half of what many believe to be the greatest songwriting partnerships of all time, he began to ruminate on what someone needs to have achieved in order to feel secure in themselves, commenting, quite hilariously, that he felt that he would have achieved enough by this stage in his life to not be nervous around anyone and yet he still was. As his words tailed off, he wondered aloud if it was just a part of the human condition to constantly ask if you are ever really good enough. If anything in this book should give you solace when you are faced with your own limitations, it should be that sometimes even Sir Paul McCartney may wonder if he is good enough.

When Liam Gallagher, frontman of British rock band Oasis, entered a cramped little space situated on the top floor of a tall and thin warren-like recording studio complex in central London, I was nervous. He is a mercurial presence and in the moments before he came through the door, I wondered which Liam Gallagher I would meet today – surly, visibly bored, non-compliant and withdrawn Liam, or open, interested and charismatic Liam. Thankfully, it was the latter. I had no notes, no earpiece in my ear to relay questions to me from a producer and no agenda other than to find out more about this enigma of a man. If it wasn't being filmed and we didn't have little clip microphones attached to our jackets, it would have been just two men on a cheap sofa having a chat about life. We started by talking about his monumental collection of parka jackets and went from there. I didn't ask him about an Oasis reunion or explicitly try to get him to talk about the long-running feud between him and his elder brother Noel. What I did do was frame the question of fraternal fallout around the effect it was having on their mother. As a son who also has an older brother, I thought about the effect such a cataclysmic and very public parting of ways would have on my mother and compared the two situations. Not because I wanted to invite him to slag off his brother – he has social media for that purpose – but because I wanted to understand what effect it was having on the matriarch of the Gallagher family. He answered that if something was to happen to his mother and the two brothers were still on bad terms, then there would be 'war'. His comments made headlines across the UK, from the *NME* to the *Daily Mail*. Ask the question, step back and listen to the answer. Listen to the response and let it trigger in you a further need to understand who this man really is and what makes him tick. To spend that limited amount of time wisely in trying to see the world through his eyes, even though they were covered by sunglasses.

Rather than trawling through the hundreds of podcasted interviews that I have conducted over the years, to write this chapter, I simply relied on those conversations that immediately sprang to mind, as these are the moments that must have had the biggest impact on me. They are examples of how my approach to the conversation has allowed the interviewees to be their most honest, expressive and, at times, vulnerable selves. In 2019, I interviewed the RADA-trained actor David Harewood, one of the stars of the huge TV series *Homeland*. He came onto my radio show to talk about a documentary he had made called *Psychosis and Me*, that dealt with his mental health battles and the terror and trauma of being sectioned when he was just twenty-three years old. Our time together on the radio had gone really well and he had been eloquent and inspiring throughout it, without ever getting upset as he recounted his largely happy childhood and then his years at the world-renowned school of acting RADA. But as a young man, his life became one of considerable struggle and he relived with candour these moments of pain caused by a breakdown in his mental health in that beautiful baritone voice of his.

As the thirty minutes were coming to an end, I asked David to think back to an image of him as a youngster that I'd seen in the documentary. This picture of David Harewood symbolised the precociousness of youth. There he stood, radiating confidence with nuclear levels of swagger. With just a suit jacket draped over his bare torso, a gold chain around his neck and a pair of black sunglasses completing the look of Arctic-like coolness, he looked ready to take on the world. I asked the actor what it felt like to look back at that picture and then to imagine reaching through time to talk to his much younger self, to place his middle-aged hands on that face and tell that young man, who stood on the precipice of opportunity but also of profound mental breakdown, that in the end it would be OK. How would it feel to be able to express to that soon-to-be deeply troubled young actor that he was not just going to survive his ordeals to come but break through the other side of them and go on to prosper in a way he could not have imagined at that earlier point in his life? As David processed this imaginary scenario, there was silence, then an audible gulp as he began to think of that young man and the destructive experiences that were about to engulf him. He broke the silence by saying, 'I wasn't expecting this,' as he struggled to deal with the enormity of what lay before the young man in the picture and his eyes showed the faintest hints of beginning to tear up. He gathered his thoughts, composed himself and then beautifully articulated where he was now in his life.

The huge sense of relief in knowing that, in the end, his career had taken off, and that the narrative arc of his life had bent towards light and not darkness, seemed to well up inside of him. He was genuinely taken aback by this hypothetical scene that I had presented him with. It had clearly unlocked in him so many emotions. It was not my intention to upset him, quite the opposite in fact, but by listening to David throughout the interview and inquiring gently, he revealed to my audience how terrifying an ordeal it had been for him and how raw it still was. After the microphone faders were pulled down and the red light in the studio went off, we shared a few moments together. He seemed genuinely exhausted and said that I had slowly opened him up like a tin can. I am not a therapist, or a psychologist, I am a conversationalist, and I had just had one of the most memorable conversations of my career. The roots of why David reacted in the way that he did to me lay with how I connected the success he had achieved later on in life with the hopes he had had as a young man. Hopes that were almost extinguished by the mental health issues that he experienced. What my experience should engender in you is the requirement to be constantly curious. Deeper conversations require more inquiry. As more is revealed, connections that would otherwise never appear rise to the surface and allow you to gently probe further.

What I believe this shows in a wider sense is how important it is to be brave and honest when asking questions. People have stories, ones they want to share. Never be reticent to ask them about their experiences of life and to be inquisitive without being intrusive. If you search out the answers because you genuinely care, then you will learn more about another person than you can imagine.

Speaking to people about loss is something we will all have to do at some point in our lives. A best friend of yours who has lost a parent, a partner who has lost a sibling or, one of the worst possible things to confront, a mother who has lost her child. I will never forget speaking to a woman called Fatima Khan in February 2014 for my BBC Asian Network phone-in show. She wasn't a film star, an award-winning author or a multimillion-selling recording artist. She was a normal mother and grandmother whose life had been changed forever. Her son was Dr Abbas Khan, a British orthopaedic surgeon who had travelled to Syria in 2012, alongside other medical professionals, to try to help the Syrian people who were in the midst of the carnage created by armed groups who fought each other with little or no regard for civilian casualties. Every week, he was criss-crossing the Turkish–Syrian border and working in a hospital to help those in need. He didn't ask which side they were on or who had hurt them, he just did what he had been taught to do and that was to help save lives. In November 2012, in a field hospital in Aleppo, then a rebel-held area, he was detained by the Syrian regime and, according to Dr Khan himself, 'accused of treating dying civilians [women and children], which has been classed as an act of terrorism'. By December 2013, he was dead. A suicide, according to the regime, but the UK Foreign Office declared that he was 'in effect murdered'.

Fatima's story was one of desperation, frustration and a crushing guilt. She was a little old lady with a lioness's heart and a mother's relentless drive to protect her child. While her son was in detention, she travelled alone to the darkest recesses of President Assad's Syrian state to try to bring her son home alive. She went to prisons, government ministries and embassies, all in the hope that she could save her child. She visited him in prison and he wept, his mind and body battered and broken by the state's torturers, pleading for his mother to save him. She could not.

As I sat in front of this mother in mourning in a radio studio in central London with microphones and screens between us, her anguish seeped from every pore. 'I live with this, and I cry all the time till I die,' she said. We are used to hearing people focus on the light of a departed soul, the joy they brought to the world and the power of hope in the midst of such turmoil. She could not. It was too soon. 'I lost my son. We are living in a very bad world.' I let her speak, left space for the silences and asked her if she wanted to stop every time she began to cry. It was my very first lesson in the art of listening to someone whose trauma had overwhelmed them, of ensuring that the questions were neither voyeuristic nor vulgar. The temptation most people have is to break the silence when placed into emotionally difficult situations. To try to find solutions, and provide respite and comfort. Faced with human pain and suffering, we look for words that will be a balm for the soul or that we can use to deflect attention away from the anguish for just a few moments in order to provide some respite from the pain. I have learned to do the opposite as a broadcaster. It is better not to jump into every silence but let those moments last as long as they need to. This is true in life as well as in broadcasting. By allowing the person in front of you to gather their thoughts and pause for as long as they need, they will be more likely to continue if that is what they wish to do. Nothing that you can say will erase the pain, but appreciating that silence is a space for further reflection is important. Think about this approach when talking to someone who has recently experienced a bereavement or a relationship breakdown and resist the urge to fill that awkward moment. I hope that I achieved the right tone that afternoon. That I was respectful and emotionally appropriate without ever being maudlin. I learned a lot that day. After the show finished, I sat in the studio and wept.

Respectfully asking a searching question always propels a dialogue forward; it is a catalyst for finding a deeper human connection. When my son was thirteen, he was invited to his first bar mitzvah. It was a really fun evening at the Goldmans' house. In the background of this family event, the England football team were playing Ukraine at the 2021 Euros and the boys were running around the garden being teenage boys, pumped up on hormones and sugar. At one point, I managed to get into a conversation with three Jewish women who were married to men at the bar mitzvah. There I was with these three powerful women in a semicircle in front of me and my first instinct was to take a risk and ask them a question which had a cultural stereotype at its core. I asked them what it was like the first time they had met their future Jewish mothers-in-law. They all looked at each other, laughed – possibly at the incisiveness, but more likely at the temerity of the question – and one of them remarked what a great question it was. I had long thought that there were so many similarities between the Asian and Jewish communities when it came to mothers and their oh-so-precious sons, so I hoped that they would see why I was asking the question. One of the ladies, knowing what I did for a living, was less surprised, as she understood that getting to the heart of a matter in the shortest possible time is what I do for a living. But there were no microphones in front of us, nor headphones clamped to my head. It was just a simple exercise in finding common ground through shared experience so that we would all get something more interesting than small talk out of our precious time together.

This is why professional conversationalists provide such an important function. We are not lifesavers or virus slayers, we have simply developed the skills needed to be able to connect to each other on a more satisfying level. Word by sincere probing word, and thought by processed thought, we are attempting to counter a narrative that encourages narcissism and division. Once we allow reasoned, respectful conversations to retreat and in their place impassioned monologues rule the roost, we have surrendered to the cult of the individual. There is a culture war afoot, of which some people fan the flames for social media shares and likes, some for monetary gain and others just get drawn into this phoney war through their own grievances and prejudices. My three-hour-long little radio club for the curiously empathetic needs to be a place where rancour and dogmatism are asked politely to pause and think before unleashing themselves upon us all.

In January 2018, the controversial psychologist Professor Jordan B. Peterson was a guest on my show. He had become a general in the culture wars for his views on gender pronouns, feminism and free speech. He had intellectually torn a Channel 4 news presenter apart and had become a poster boy for the anti-woke, alt-right set, who now had an intellectual heavyweight to articulate how they felt in an academic way, replete with what some regarded as cherry-picked facts, data and research. These elements gave Professor Peterson an automatic head start over all but the most intellectually rigorous people willing to take him on. His book *12 Rules for Life: An Antidote to Chaos* became an international bestseller and propelled him into a sphere of stardom rarely experienced by academics.

Prior to our conversation, I had read an interview with Professor Peterson where the interviewer had described how emotional Peterson had become when discussing the plight of a group of young men that he had spoken to after giving a lecture. Of the thousand people who had turned up to this particular presentation, around a half stayed behind afterwards to talk to him. As he began to recount what he had experienced that evening, the reporter noted that Professor Peterson's voice had begun to get even higher-pitched than usual and faltered as he battled with these emotions. In my subsequent interview with Professor Peterson, he told me, 'It's so sad that so many of these men have not had a single encouraging bloody word their entire lives. It just takes a little bit of encouragement. It's just a catastrophe that that's so rare in their lives.' This is a man who, under all the intellectual bravado, is ultimately still a clinical psychologist.

After listening back to my own interview with Professor Peterson, the algorithm that presumes to know my tastes threw me down the rabbit hole of YouTube clips that heralded triumphantly his victories in the culture wars, with such titles as 'Jordan B. Peterson vs feminism', 'vs political correctness' and 'vs social justice warriors'. He had become a clickbait generator and an engine of anger, edited and packaged to taunt liberals and excite right-wingers. As the culture war raged around him, and brought him worldwide fame and notoriety, I couldn't forget the emotional reaction he'd had when discussing the plight of young men. Beyond the noise of verbal combat, it was this aspect of Peterson's work that I wanted to explore further.

So, in October 2018, I was given the opportunity to interview him for a second time, but on this occasion not in a radio studio. My radio show's production team brought together a small gathering of men with the express purpose of trying to discover what Professor Peterson would do if we simply asked him to speak with a small group of young men. The intimate gathering was made up of individuals who'd all had very different lives, some of which involved addiction, abuse and neglect. We picked the Moss Side Fire Station Boxing Club in Manchester, run by the indomitable and thoroughly inspiring Nigel Travis, as the venue for this conversation because it personified the struggle of people who have had to overcome barriers, both personal and societal, in order to find a sense of personal responsibility, self-respect, discipline and focus. What transpired was a fascinating insight into the power of talking and listening. These were conversations devoid of conflict, agenda or malice. The whole morning was contrived, in the sense that it was for a radio show and journalists had been involved in selecting the men in attendance, but the series of dialogues that took place that day were free of the chains of the so-called culture war.

If you are of a certain political standpoint, you will find some of what Professor Peterson writes about and says deeply problematic and it is not my intention here to either defend or attack him for his views. As I sat next to him in that boxing gym, I wanted to see how he interacted with the kinds of men who had hung back that night post-lecture to converse with him. I wanted to see who he was when he was away from the histrionics of his detractors and baying smugness of his supporters, when he was required to listen and share, more than attack and defend. What would this man, who was both venerated and loathed in equal measure, be like when not being interrogated, interrupted and goaded? What Professor Jordan B. Peterson would we see?

There was a moment in the conversation when he asked a young man from the north-east of England what he thought the consequences were of not having seen his father between the ages of eight and twenty-eight. The man replied that his father would not have been a great role model if he had stuck around, due to him being violent. He then recounted a story he had been told about his father. 'When I was a child, I was sat reading a book, and it would have been a picture book, and my father picked it up and cracked it across my head and said, "What are you reading that for?"' Professor Peterson looked genuinely concerned as he began to articulate just how destructive that small dismissive act was and the repercussions of acting in such a way, quoting the German philosopher Nietzsche: 'Nietzsche said that if you want to punish someone, you should punish them for their virtues. So you wait until you see them doing something good and then you hurt them for that. Brutal man.' This was Peterson with the armour stripped away, relating his clinical experience and knowledge of philosophy in response to the ordeal of a young man sitting less that ten feet away from him. It was light, not noise.

The field of clinical psychology fascinates me because it involves having the most intimate and potentially life-changing conversations of all. Those who choose this career path devote their working lives to talking and listening to some of society's most troubled individuals. They are presented with the most disturbing aspects of the human condition and use their expertise, training and empathy to peel back layer after layer of a person's life in order to uncover what traumas lie buried deep within and then attempt to connect them to behaviours present in their lives today. These psychological wounds can manifest themselves in a myriad of different conditions, such as anxiety, psychosis, depression, eating disorders and addiction. It is hard to overemphasise the importance of the choice of words used by a qualified clinician, or the listening skills that they employ to help some of the most vulnerable people in our society.

The father of psychoanalysis is undoubtedly Sigmund Freud, who formulated his ideas in the 1890s around how our childhoods have an effect on our adult lives. He believed that a dialogue between the patient and the psychoanalyst is necessary to explore the links between our youthful agonies and adult behaviours. A dialogue in this context is not what we would usually describe an exchange of pleasantries, ideas and opinions; rather, for

Freud, it meant the patient being able to 'free-associate', or speak without the constraints of politeness, the need to make sense or, indeed, even the requirement to focus on what they are saying. The purpose of this approach was to allow the patient complete freedom to explore their thoughts, even if that meant a string of seemingly unrelated words spilled out from his or her mind into the air. According to Freud, it was essential to allow the patient to roam throughout his or her subconscious without fear of judgement or censure. The psychoanalyst would play no active part in directing the conversation and make no attempt to problem-solve. By deliberately stepping back from trying to intervene, it was thought that the analyst would enable their patient to uncover associations and deeply embedded feelings that may lay otherwise stubbornly out of sight.

Freud believed that the process he developed avoided three issues that can occur in therapy. The first being 'transference', whereby a person transfers the feelings they have from one person to another. An example of this could be a person who mistrusts another simply because they remind them of someone they were once in a relationship with. Another example could be transferring the feelings you had about your parents onto a partner or your children. The second issue that Freud wished to avoid was that of 'projection', which is where we project our own qualities or experiences onto someone else. These could be unwanted character traits in yourself that, rather than face, you end up attributing to someone else. A graphic and all-too-familiar example of projection would be where a school bully is projecting their own insecurities onto their victims. The third issue is 'resistance', which is where we block out particular memories and feelings, often because of shame.

While Freudian free association is rarely used in modern psychoanalysis, when it comes to the subject of this book, it is fascinating to note the themes of non-judgement, listening without attempting to fix, patience and open-mindedness. These methods are as relevant today as they were over a century ago when it comes to confronting difficult things. It is hardly revelatory to point out that we do not relish the idea of having challenging conversations. To avoid an issue rather than meet it head on is most people's default setting. We have all at some point in our lives tried to avoid having to deliver some home truths or be the bearer of bad news. But the job of the clinical psychologist and psychoanalyst is to have nothing but deeply challenging conversations. Interestingly, you will notice some crossover between chapter six, 'Conversations in Extremis', and here, where I will be showcasing the skills of others who have made conversation a central pillar of their professional identity. My time spent with the former President of Ireland Mary McAleese speaking about the Irish peace process, the film-maker Deeyah Khan and her extraordinary time spent with American white supremacists and the former police crisis negotiator John Sutherland bore a lot of commonalities. Those crossovers include what inspiration we can glean from people who

229

in their professional lives rely heavily on their command of language, the astuteness with which they assess a situation and how intensely they care about what is being said to them.

14

Professor Tanya Byron:
Why Conversations Fail

There are over 37,000 psychologists working across the United Kingdom, but when it came to the world of clinical psychology, there was only one person I wanted to speak to. Not simply because she is a chartered clinical psychologist, a professor in the public understanding of science and boasts an academic résumé even my parents would be proud of, but most importantly, she has an extraordinary ability to connect with people of all backgrounds. Away from the clinic, the lecture theatre and the radio and TV studios where she is often asked to provide expert analysis on a range of mental health issues, it was her podcast 'How Did We Get Here?' which she co-presents with her close friend TV presenter Claudia Winkleman, that really showcases her incisive questioning and how attuned she is to deconstructing the problems of others. Alongside her brilliant podcast, Professor Byron has been writing a weekly column in *The*

Times newspaper for seventeen years. Over that period of time, she has answered letters from readers dealing with domestic violence, depression, eating disorders, sexual dysfunction and a range of significant mental health challenges.

The first question I asked her was what her professional training had taught her about having conversations, specifically in the early stages of her career. She explained that at first the overriding urge was to try to rescue everybody. Professor Byron had grown up in a home where her father had had mental health issues. She was at pains to say how amazing her successful filmmaker father was, a person who she loved dearly, but his moods would fluctuate wildly. At times, he could be a joy to be around, but he was a man who, with the benefit of hindsight, was clinically anxious and at times depressed. With these events playing out in the background and foreground of her life, it is no wonder Professor Byron approached her clinical studies with a crusading zeal to fix those who came into her clinical orbit. By her own admission, this overwhelming belief that she could solve every problem prevented her initially from listening closely enough to what her patients were saying. In time, she had to learn to quieten what was going on inside of her in order to be able to hear what was going on in the minds of others.

Professor Byron believes that conversations fail because we become preoccupied with what she calls our 'internal monologue', which focuses on what we want people to hear us say, instead of attempting to comprehend what is being said to us. She singles out social media as a glaring example of our internal monologues holding sway over everything else. 'There's no thoughtfulness, there's no empathy for another person's position and that for me, I think, is the key.' There is also a fear of seeking out other views that are at the edges of our understanding or even tolerance because we are genuinely scared to ask questions, terrified that they may be misconstrued as statements in disguise.

Professor Byron laments what she sees as the perniciousness of cancel culture: 'What worries me so much is the beauty of debate is being lost. Sometimes you have to ask really difficult, sometimes quite outrageous questions in order to understand the parameters of an issue. Now you ask a question and you're cancelled.' Professor Byron believes that rather than simply cancelling such people, we have to discover if they are willing to change their opinions, and if so, we have to find a way to listen to them. 'We're becoming more polarised because we can't tolerate these difficult conversations.'

Attempting to understand the motivations of those who inhabit an ideological space that exists far away from the one that you live in is often difficult. It requires patience and self-awareness, but ultimately it provides us with a much clearer picture of our own views and prejudices. Like me, I suspect that what she revels in is the challenge of trying to grasp what it is that makes people tick, though her role involves the kind of pressures that a radio presenter doesn't have to contend with. Tanya said that she thinks she and I share some characteristics: 'We're fundamentally very nosy people. We're fascinated by the detail of other people's lives.' She provided further proof that at a very basic level there are similarities between our two jobs because they are both about talking to people with purpose: 'People are not just providing a conversation, they're providing a conversation with intent.'

In the course of having a conversation with intent, Professor Byron revealed one of her driving forces is the need to try to comprehend why some people do really bad things. This curiosity began when she was fifteen years old and her grandmother was murdered. The 'bad things' being some of the worst crimes that humans can inflict upon each other. What if you were tasked with talking to someone who is 'sexually attracted to children'? As Professor Byron uttered those words, she noticed my reaction on our Zoom call immediately. 'I can see your face now when I am saying it, reacting to the idea of having that conversation and thinking about it, in order to try to understand how to stop it and to stop children being abused.'

Imagine having to share a space and a conversation with a person who has committed one of the most reprehensible acts of criminality known to society. A clinical psychologist may need to have an exchange with them in order to decipher the complex variety of reasons that led to them committing these vile acts and to prevent them happening again. She was keen to stress that this has to be done as part of working with children who disclose their abuse and also as part of the criminal justice process: of arrest, trial and, if found guilty, conviction – which also, sadly, means often a child will be abused in order for a perpetrator to receive any kind of treatment. The work that she and others carry out is not designed to undermine a prosecution or find justification for the crimes committed, as some may choose to frame it. She is all too aware of how emotionally charged such work is, for clinician and patient but also in light of public perceptions regarding the very point of doing such work in the first place. If Tanya Byron uses the word 'understand', then some people may wrongly assume that the psychologist in question is engaged in showing understanding to a paedophile. She acknowledges the hysteria this causes, when individuals and groups accuse those involved in the treatment of sex offenders of attempting to make excuses for immoral and unlawful acts against children. Nothing could be further from the truth. Simply shouting 'Lock them up and throw away the key!' does not reflect the reality of the criminal justice system. The majority of people who commit these heinous crimes will be released from prison one day, some will reoffend.

Of the 87,000 prisoners currently held in prisons across the UK (2021), nearly 13,000 are classed as sex offenders. Across the entire prison population, there are only approximately sixty prisoners on a whole-life tariff, meaning they have no possibility of ever being released on parole or any other form of conditional release. So the vast majority of those in UK prisons will eventually be released back out into the world, paedophiles included. With these facts at our disposal, we need people who are willing to attempt to treat those who abuse children, because the likelihood is that they will walk among us again. If there is a prospect that some can be prevented from reoffending and children spared from this abuse, then the work should be supported and not vilified.

It is clearly an issue that Professor Byron has had to face head on and her response was as lucid as it was logical: 'I don't think understanding something is condoning it. I think understanding something is trying to find ways to change it and make sure it doesn't ever happen again.' She then explained what the purpose of understanding is. 'We can try to enable you to make sure that whatever it is that compels you to do that can be addressed, so you don't go on and do it again. So understanding is fundamentally important to change. People who abuse children don't get locked up for the rest of their lives. So as soon as they're out, if we don't understand, if we don't intervene, if we don't know what to do, it could happen again. And this is the issue.' In having difficult conversations of this nature, the urge to dismiss out of hand what you are hearing is especially pronounced when discussing the clinical treatment of paedophiles. It is not uncommon or illogical for people to demand that this particular type of criminal, one who poses a threat to our children, is locked up for life, but that is not the reality of the system that tries, convicts and locks up the guilty.

Tanya chose her words carefully when describing how she must approach the work: 'The conversation is about courage. It's about holding onto one's own feelings, strong feelings, and I have very strong feelings of anger and disgust about children who are abused.' Again and again, she hammered the point home. 'There are some people who don't want to change, who believe that this is what should be done. Those people are a risk. And one has to think very carefully about how they're supervised when they're not incarcerated. But there are people who do want to change and there are people who don't want to offend or reoffend.' As she eloquently and passionately argued for the need to prevent these people from offending/reoffending, she briefly outlined the inherent difficulties within the process itself. Firstly, a person in her position has to be able to differentiate between someone who has no intention of stopping and a person who does. From there, you need to clarify if you have made the right decision and then it is all down to what happens next.

I was curious as to how you even begin a conversation with someone who has been found guilty of crimes that would quite literally make your skin crawl, whether you were in their immediate vicinity or not. This is where the language gets really tricky and can be misinterpreted. 'If I want to have a meaningful conversation, I've got to be able to be decent in order for them to be able to talk to me.' She also discussed the role of empathy. This isn't, after all, a self-harming teenager or a person with an eating disorder, whose cases would naturally elicit empathy. Many would find the idea that empathy could be part of a conversation with an abuser of children very difficult to accept.

To try to explain how empathy comes into this situation, she framed our conversation around how she would attempt, in simplistic terms, to build an empathetic connection with me. 'As a white woman, I think how awful it must be to grow up and people always be mean to you because of the colour of your skin.' This is a relatively straightforward example of how two people could find common ground. She was not trying to claim she would know how that feels but to empathise with how terrible it would be to have to go through that. It is an example that few could take any issue with. Yet she is all too aware that once she even introduces the concept of empathy into a conversation with a paedophile, a line is crossed. She delivered her explanation with a clinician's manner but also with the experience of someone in the public eye who has incurred the wrath of some for speaking publicly about these issues: 'I empathise with the fact that that person is in a situation where they are behaving in ways that are damaging to them, but more importantly damaging to others, particularly children.' She reiterated the importance of courage when addressing these taboos but also how, without these conversations, we may be faced with more children having to live with the trauma of abuse – if we don't understand how to prevent it, more children will be abused. This is a significant aspect of child protection but one very few are prepared to think about, given the emotions that surround the behaviour of paedophiles. She is adamant that it is right and proper to do so: 'I really believe the only way we can make changes is to have the courage to talk about the most difficult aspects of things that need to change.'

Professor Byron sits on the board of the NSPCC (the National Society for the Prevention of Cruelty to Children), so it is an area that she is hugely knowledgeable and passionate about and, alongside her colleagues, she has spent much of her career pouring her efforts into protecting children from situations in which they face abuse. She asked, 'If I can't have conversations with people who abuse children, if I can't understand why they do that, if there is not full provision of services to those people, how do we stop it happening?' She then quoted Dostoyevsky: 'Nothing is easier than to denounce the evildoer; nothing is more difficult than to understand him.'

This is a book about having better conversations, but that doesn't mean solely positive ones. Professor Tanya Byron has years of clinical experience to draw upon and we do not, but that doesn't mean that we cannot employ some of the techniques that she uses to navigate our way through some of life's more challenging dialogues. When we take a strong emotional position in an exchange, Professor Byron would advise us all to stop and think about why it is affecting us at such a level. The self-awareness needed here to self-critique and not project your own frustrations onto another is an important part of this. As a clinical psychologist, Professor Byron talks about 'pacing', 'being grounded' and 'being in the moment' in order to show that you empathise because you have really listened, but at the same time acknowledging that you cannot fully understand a set of experiences that are alien to your own. How can a white person know what it really feels like to be a person of colour, or a man admit to having had the same lived experience as a woman?

Professor Byron uses the word 'understand' with very specific boundaries attached. She understands that past traumas have ramifications that can lead to a person seeking out professional help. She understands that that is enough to open up the conversation. But in building that connection, it is equally important to admit what you don't know. 'I would never disrespect you by saying I understand how you feel, because I've not been through what you've been through. We've got to be able to say that no one's an expert on everything.'

We then began a conversation about a more general and far less contentious subject: curiosity. All of the people who I interviewed for this book are naturally curious, perhaps supernaturally so. Are they an exclusive club of inquisitorial outliers predisposed to peer into the lives of others and find human connection? Or is such a desire to connect available to all of us and all that is needed is the willingness to develop the skill set required?

First and foremost, if we do not take an interest in the lives of others, how will we be capable of truly understanding the world around us? Professor Byron believes that as we grow older our curiosity subsides, but rather than a natural degeneration, she thinks that it is effectively educated out of our consciousness. As children get older and move into adulthood, she contends that they become less curious, more polarised and less interested. She did not mince her words when she said, 'I think our education system does everything to drive a natural instinct to be curious out of us.' In the UK, our education system is 'built on targets and testing around a curriculum where you have to learn certain things, and you have to be able to answer questions to a marking scheme'. The result of this approach is generation after generation of children being taught how to display that they have learned a subject to a sufficient degree to be awarded a grade for doing so. As far as Professor Byron is concerned, this system of learning 'completely sits against curiosity'.

There is an alternative approach and she was keen to stress that there are innovations in education that inject curiosity back into the lives of students. One such innovation is 'flipped learning'. The orthodox school day involves your wonderful child sitting in the classroom while the teacher feeds them information which they then bring home to analyse and decipher, also known as homework. When you flip this approach, the teacher is no longer the info spreader-in-chief (not a pedagogical term) and the student constructs their own understanding of a subject away from the classroom. Once back in the class, what is absorbed elsewhere is then aided and encouraged by discussion and focused guidance from a teacher.

Even the space within the classroom is changed to accommodate different styles of learning, whether that's in groups huddled together debating the effects of the naval blockade on Germany and Austria–Hungary on the course of the First World War or sitting alone in a corner cogitating on complicated algebraic conundrums. Flipped learning prioritises inquisitiveness and the importance of having open and invigorating discussions fuelled by a child's ownership of their learning and, most importantly, a constant nurturing of their curiosity. This is the opposite of a child rote learning, then regurgitating a flurry of facts. Putting the child at the centre of their own education and encouraging them to self-analyse and have the freedom to express their ideas isn't a million miles away from how Professor Byron addressed her own working practices: 'That's kind of how I would work with a patient, you see. So it gets back to curiosity and how you ask a question.'

Professor Byron also believes that there are some basic foundations which we could all address in order to be better at communicating with each other. For one, we need to learn how to be quieter. Not in the sense of tip-toeing around a library or fearing to disturb a just-settled baby. The quietness she asks for is that which provides an opportunity to listen rather than talk simply for the sake of it. 'It's too much noise,' she explained. 'You say this, I've got to tell you what I think.' Every answer is an invitation to exhibit another nugget of gold from your own mind and not a catalyst for further investigation. What Professor Byron wants to see more of is self-analysis, not automatic projection. If a person says something you disagree with, rather than dismissing them out of hand and going on the offensive to explain your own thoughts, think about why you are struggling with what they had to say and ask them what forms the foundations of their thinking.

When I interviewed the brilliant author and journalist Johann Hari for chapter three of this book, one of the stories he told me related to an encounter he had after absconding to a sleepy little place called Provincetown, New England, which for most of the year had a population that barely touched 4,000 inhabitants, but in the summer its population swelled to almost twenty times that. He was there for the purposes of trying to regenerate his ability to focus in all spheres of his life. While there, he became involved in conversation with a British man, who went on a rant about how he thought all Brexit voters were racist idiots and boasted proudly of how he no longer spoke to his stepfather because he had voted for the UK to exit the European Union. He was playing to the gallery, assuming that the Remain-voting Johann would high-five him upon hearing of this familial excommunication. But if this man was expecting a show of Brexiteer-hating solidarity, then he was sadly disappointed by Johann's response.

As a staunch Remainer, rather than being closed off to a Leaver's motives, curiosity led Johann towards wanting to know what had compelled the man's stepfather to vote Leave in the referendum. He asked him if he knew why his stepfather had made that decision and, unsurprisingly, the man said he didn't know and didn't care. The journalist, the author and the human being found this answer deeply troubling, although entirely predictable. Granted, if it were to have taken place, it would not have been an easy conversation for stepson and stepfather, but the fact it never took place at all symbolises one of the great issues of our age – the embracing of partisanship and placing of trust in perfidious prophets of doom who would rather sow division than encourage unity. Just imagine if the belligerent chap had expressed an interest in his stepfather's beliefs in a genuinely open way. What could they both have learned from such an exchange? The goal would not have been to try to change each other but to attempt to understand one another.

As our own conversation drew to a close, I asked Professor Byron if she was optimistic that we can learn to place more value and importance on having better conversations. She acknowledged that the pandemic had changed how we were able to communicate with each other, particularly while lockdowns were in place, and through that, we realised how much we all missed each other, discovering that the virtual conversation was no replacement for the face-to-face one. She also wanted to point out that conversation changes. Referring to how her now grown-up children operate in both the online and offline world, and the bonds they have with their friends and the conversations they are having, she ended on a positive note, saying, 'It all sounds pretty good to me.'

15

Lorraine Kelly:
How to be More Curious

The space created for a radio conversation lacks the bells and whistles of a television studio. There's no need for a team of camera operatives, lighting, sound engineers or a floor manager. Nobody suddenly appears to dab your forehead with a bit of powder and check your hair is in place during a short break. There isn't a director yelling 'cut' because someone has left a branded can of drink in the background. Radio presenters don't have to wait until the cameras change position or for the autocue to be edited because somebody put a question mark after my surname and I signed off by questioning my own name. In a radio interview setting, there are usually just the two of you and, while it may not be the most natural of surroundings, it does lend itself to the kind of environment needed in order for a more revealing encounter to take place. So no matter how famous the face, the voice, or the artistry, the conversation comes first.

LET'S TALK

Recently, a listener to my show tweeted this, and the reason I mention it is because it was the first time I had seen someone so concisely describe on social media what I do: 'It's the quality of his first question on any topic and then, importantly, his follow-up Qs which are in turn driven by his strong listening skills. He doesn't seem to have a list of Qs to get through: it comes across as an in-depth conversation.' If you wanted to read a succinct description of how I embark on every interview, that is it.

But just because you do the job of an interviewer, either on TV or radio, that doesn't necessarily make you a conversationalist. A newsreader or reporter in situ may have just a few minutes to ask a set of pre-written questions and then will have to move on to another story or throw back to the presenter in the studio. In political and current affairs journalism in particular, you will find countless media heavyweights who may have more time with their interviewees but their style is more gladiatorial, so it is less of a conversation and more of an interrogation. You will be familiar with such a spectacle, which gives the wide-eyed crowds surrounding the bear pit the chance to have their bloodlust satiated as another hapless minister trips up over his own words, relays dreamed-up statistics or attempts to answer a question by not answering it, twelve times. Then there is the interview as pure entertainment. In this format, rather than delving into the psyche of a guest or trying to expose their hypocrisy, the audience is presented with what they want, which is a side-splittingly funny parade of anecdotes. In the authored documentary

248

corner, which means there is a presenter fronting their own film, sometimes a gentle, almost invisible interlocutor is needed, who simply nudges a guest along with curiosity but gives nothing of themselves. All of these require skill and the very best in each discipline are widely lauded for their talents.

On every channel, there are those whose job it is to interview people for a living and there are many people I could have approached who would have been able to make a fascinating contribution to these pages. But after appearing on my show in December 2019 to talk about her book *Shine*, it became clear to me that Lorraine Kelly had to be part of the book – even if, at that stage, it was just a set of ideas in my head.

Every weekday morning at 9 a.m. on ITV, Lorraine hosts a live show that involves a wide range of topics, life stories and reminiscences with actors, authors, musicians, celebrities and members of the public. Her journalistic training means that she never shies away from discussing deeply sensitive stories from people who have experienced heartbreak and trauma, and performed extraordinary feats of human bravery. Of all the morning TV present-ers who ply their trade, Lorraine Kelly is the one with whom I most identify. When Lorraine sits in front of a guest, whoever they are and from whatever background they happen to be from, she is so relaxed and engaged. Whether it be a movie star or a mother with a personal story to tell, her methodology of listening with interest and empathy clearly works. Her interviews are both inquisitive and endearing. As a viewee, when you turn on the TV in the morning wanting to be eased into the day while sipping tea from your favourite mug, you want to see an interviewer who isn't grandstanding and constantly making it about them at the expense of their guest. You want to feel as though you are earwigging in on a chat between friends. This is what a morning spent watching Lorraine Kelly on ITV feels like. She has honed the ability to be able to ask even the most difficult questions in a disarmingly charming way.

I cannot quite explain what it felt like to be having a Zoom catch-up with a woman who has been on our morning TV screens for over thirty years. It is this intimate, conversational style of hers that means we all feel that we know Lorraine – and even more, that she is a woman we would want to hang out with, or pour our troubles out to. It is no surprise then that even with the deadening effect of a computer screen, she radiated warmth and openness. The approach she employs illustrates a curiosity that doesn't hinge upon getting a headline in a tabloid or hoping that a video clip will go viral, but shows a genuine interest in her guest. Though there's no doubt that Lorraine would baulk at the use of the words 'approach' and 'employs', because who you see on your TV screens is the same Lorraine Kelly that you may meet in a supermarket aisle or in a restaurant. 'It's one of the few jobs you can be yourself. You're not light entertainment with jazz hands and a burly bow tie,' she said. 'You're just you and that is a privilege.'

As a child, she was encouraged by her parents to query the world around her. Even before Lorraine started school, her mother and father made sure that she could both read and write. By her own admission, she has always been a 'blether' or chatterbox. The journalist and TV presenter fondly recounted being bought a telescope by her father after they had watched the moon landings together. She was only five years old, but it was emblematic of how a spirit of inquiry was engendered in both her brother and her from a very young age.

Alongside an encouragement to question the world around, Lorraine's father also made sure that both of his children treated all people the same by often quoting an old Scottish phrase: 'We're all Jock Tamson's bairns.' It is an expression that loosely translates as 'we are all the human race.' They are words that remain with her to this day and, even though she admits to being saddled by 'that working-class cringe', she regards all the exchanges that take place on her show to be of equal value, regardless of the power, the fame or the status of the person seated opposite her. Those in the media who believe that the combative approach to interviewing eclipses the gentler method of extracting information from a guest have never seen Lorraine ply her trade. 'I am not into that sort of gladiatorial style,' she said. 'I always think, as my granny said, "You get more with sugar than vinegar," and you do.'

Within the first few minutes of speaking to this bona fide legend, I knew that I had made the right choice in inviting her to be part of *Let's Talk* because she knows exactly who she is and what she is trying to achieve. 'For the kind of show that I do, I think it should be a conversation.' She also reinforces the principle that so many in this book are keen to focus on when it comes to talking to each other – the importance of listening. She remembers the times that she has been the interviewee and recognised immediately that the questioner is sticking to the pre-written questions and not listening to the answers. According to Lorraine, the actor Michael Gambon once told an interviewer that he was gay but had to give it up because it made his eyes water 'to prove the interviewer wasn't listening to him'. Try that next time you are convinced that someone isn't listening to you in a conversation. Or if plagiarism isn't your thing, make up your own outlandish story to insert at the opportune moment. I may try telling an unsuspecting journalist who I suspect isn't entirely engaged in what I have to say that I had to give up a career in the military to become a DJ because I was found to be bulletproof and the other soldiers didn't think that it was fair, and see where that gets me.

Alongside the significance of listening, it is imperative that we never lose – or we seek to recover – that curiosity which will enable us to have better conversations. She recalled an event at the National Geographic Society where the guest speaker was Michael Palin. He told the assembled audience that 'the best thing about a human being is never losing that curiosity'. It is no surprise to me that Lorraine then went on to say, 'I'm curious about everything.'

But working in a TV format where curiosity is encouraged and listening is essential doesn't shield Lorraine from what is happening in the wider world. She noted, 'We're losing the art of conversation, which is a great shame . . . because communication is what makes us human beings.' She honed in on Twitter as a place of division and toxicity, and asks a question fundamental to the very reason for writing this book: 'People are at opposite ends throwing rocks at one another. When did that become the norm?'

The central premise of *Let's Talk* is that this needn't and shouldn't be the norm, and that there are tools at our disposal that we must actively employ in order to prevent the rock-throwing from becoming the received order of things. If we are to escape the silos we have built for ourselves, or had imposed upon us, we simply have to speak to each other. Rather than rely on news reports, ranty polemics, editorials, tweets or Facebook pages to help you form an impression of someone, the significance of spending time with another person exchanging views in a calm and mutually respectful way cannot be overestimated. Whether that be on a successful TV chat show, in a workplace, a school playground or in a social circle, Lorraine says, 'How can you possibly understand someone who's of a different religion, or different sexuality, if you don't sit and talk to them?'

This may seem like a utopian dream if you live in an entirely monocultural environment, but few actually do. All around you, there is a diversity of histories, memories and opinions that you have not tapped into. Think about the people who surround you and prepare yourself to dig a little deeper when next the opportunity presents itself. This will require some courage on your part, but generate that curiosity to go beyond the superficial and strive to discover more about those who are in your immediate orbit. From there, you can explore the further edges of your social universe.

As I write out these words, I begin to ask myself how well I really know some of the people I regard to be close friends. What are their attitudes to religion and to gender equality? What complexities lay beneath the exterior coating? What of their childhoods, their teenage years, the time spent before we met that shaped them into the ready-made item that came packaged for friendship? Writing is revelatory to both producer and consumer and this process has inspired me to discover even more about those who are close to me. The only way that we are going to achieve genuine closeness is to have better conversations with each other. These relationships provide an anchor to keep us steady in choppy waters, a refuge to dwell in when insecurities abound and a resting place to find solace in shared instances of joy and sadness.

When a person sits down to watch Lorraine Kelly on the telly, there is a conversational communion that takes place, as a celebrity opens up with a relatability that endears and inspires, a story of heroism or tragedy that places our own lives into context, or the simple task of learning from a stranger that we are not alone in the struggles we face.

*

This section has focused upon two professional conversationalists who perform very different roles in their chosen fields. Both are in the public eye and both are extremely good at their jobs. From conversations that can have life-or-death outcomes to those that provide entertainment, those qualities of listening, curiosity, giving space to the other person to express themselves and actively listening with huge reserves of empathy bond Professor Tanya Byron and Lorraine Kelly together.

Professor Byron has spent years training to be able to have dialogues that not only need to produce measurable outcomes but also to be constantly aware of the risks involved and the duty of care she has to the recipients of her expertise. When Lorraine has a guest seated before her, she has to 'make sure that they feel comfortable and that they can trust you'. For one, it is an endeavour that has involved decades of study and hands-on experience; for the other, it is a role that relies more on instinct than self-analysis. On one hand, Lorraine maintains, 'If I over-analyse it, it will disappear.' But when asked what makes a great conversation, she is all too aware of the mechanics: 'It should be like a really good game of tennis, with both sides listening and batting the subject backwards and forwards and not being too scared to ask a difficult question.'

As our time together drew to an end, Lorraine told me about the one superpower she would like to have. Understandably, she chose one that would make her not only the best at what she does in the UK but cement her status as a global icon of calm and measured conversation. 'I would want to be able to speak every single language.'

Speaking to these two amazing women has reminded me that we possess this superpower in abundance already. It may not involve fluency in Sinhalese or Cantonese, German or Punjabi, but empathy, curiosity and the ability to listen does provide a universality of communication, because wherever you are in the world, an openness to engage is an invitation to connect, and that begins with a conversation.

CONCLUSION

When I began writing this book, I thought about the near past, present and the future of conversation. The near past and present have been influenced heavily by the inexorable ascent of technology and social media, which has in turn had a big impact on how we communicate with each other. But I also considered how the last decade has shaped my own attitude towards the art of conversation, ever since becoming a full-time speech radio broadcaster and in light of the feedback I receive from a large mainstream audience. The writing of *Let's Talk* led to me digging in the crates of my own memory to unearth moments of wonder.

At the BBC Asian Network and then at BBC Radio 5 Live, I have conducted interviews that left an indelible mark on me and they immediately sprang to mind when preparing to sit down and write this book. Through the broadcasting, hosting and podcasting work that I carry out today, I am blessed to have the opportunity to speak with so many interesting individuals and delve into their worlds. You have met a few such people within the pages of this book and I hope that you have found their experiences, observations and advice thought-provoking and instructive.

What I had not taken much notice of as I forged on with my broadcasting career was the evolution of conversation and how the very act of being able to converse eloquently and with relevancy was once considered an art form in everyday life. From the ancient Greeks to the denizens of London's eighteenth-century coffee shops, people valued the ability to speak and listen, elucidate and illuminate, and elevate each other to new levels of intellectual inquiry through the exchange of ideas. Value was placed on the words spoken by an individual, not simply to boast to the world of their own formidable powers in this area, but to have their views challenged and refined by dialogue and debate.

In Stephen Miller's excellent book *Conversation: A History of a Declining Art*, a chapter is devoted to the much-vaunted eighteenth-century man of letters Dr Samuel Johnson, who was regarded as one of the greatest conversationalists of his age, though he also had his fair share of contemporary detractors. Miller writes that Dr Johnson believed that those who excelled in the art of conversation should have their views refined through challenge, but that such people couldn't help but attract both envy and even hatred for being so adept in the art form.

As Johnson himself wrote, 'There is nothing by which a man exasperates most people more, than by displaying a superior ability or brilliancy in conversation.' But *Let's Talk* isn't a book designed to segregate the purveyors of highfalutin conversational ideals from those who would rather stare at a screen and mutter incoherently when the Wi-Fi stops working. I sincerely hope that this passion project of mine will act as a catalyst for self-analysis but not a reason to feel insecure about your own capabilities in what Miller describes as 'the conversible world'. The world of conversation should not purely revolve around an exalted impression of what constitutes an exchange of words.

Miller goes on to explain that Dr Johnson felt that if eighteenth-century English society expected everybody to speak with more 'elegance, purity and truth', underpinned by a broad and impressive vocabulary, then they would be sorely disappointed. Expecting such high standards and attaching social status to conversational skills would allow snobbery, sarcasm and impoliteness to creep in, directed at those who did not meet the mark. In a society that was beginning to embrace the newly fashionable concept of politeness, it was feared that this would cause some to withdraw from conversation altogether. Through the lowering of such expectations, Dr Johnson felt that those around him would actually enjoy a conversation more. Miller believes that what Dr Johnson wanted was for people to engage rather than withdraw because, as he points out, Johnson believed that to retreat from conversation would have ramifications for a person's mental faculties. If you are left feeling overwhelmed by the prospect of having to sharpen up your conversational act for fear of falling foul of the speech police, then do not worry, just remind yourself of Dr Johnson's sentiments. You have the time and you now have the tools, but what you need more than anything is the patience and the will to train yourself to be better at speaking and listening.

Conversation isn't a form of communication that just happens to you. What I learned in the course of speaking to Professor Elizabeth Stokoe was that we have agency in how we shape a dialogue and how we make others feel within it. Her example of both ordering a coffee and receiving a Wi-Fi code simultaneously instead of having to ask for it being a simple example of how a dialogue can be brief and effective. In a dialogue, the ideal process of getting from point A to point B in the most frictionless way made me think about how often our social interactions fail to do this. We should all reflect on the imagery that Professor Stokoe created of the dog owner chasing their furry friend around the field rather than both hound and human traversing it in a direct and efficient manner along a straight path. We are not automatons, so I am not suggesting that we solely communicate in a way that is devoid of the tangents that new thoughts can set us off on. What we must be aware of, though, is that the power contained within a conversation is derived from the clarity both parties bring to the exchange, even if they are not satisfied with the outcome.

CONCLUSION

As you must be aware by now, this book hasn't been purely for your benefit. The preceding words have undoubtedly given me much to think about in regard to how I approach time spent with another person. I now have words for that which I previously did instinctively. Turn taking, active listening and space-giving are vital components of an exchange, ones that should be regarded as sacrosanct if we are to truly benefit from time spent together. These are not difficult concepts to understand or act upon. Having written *Let's Talk*, I have begun to notice just how poor some people, myself included on occasion, are at applying these principles. As Dr Johnson once advised, though, I should not expect every person I meet to be a professional conversationalist, therein only disappointment lies.

Professor Stokoe described the variety of clothes that hang from the coat hanger which is the structural basis of a conversation. The garments draped on the hanger are the languages, accents and grammar that are as diverse as the cultures that are spread across planet Earth. Such exchanges can be funny, inane, deep, superficial, serious, exploratory or intimate, but all require a structure to be effective for both speaker and listener. The further I went into this subject matter, the more I saw myself as an evangelist for setting yourself to receive rather than continually transmit for the benefit of all involved.

Choosing to pay attention to the spoken words of others does not mean you are automatically appeasing the ideas of others, however. Learning about the mechanics of a conversation encouraged me to be conscious of the idea of personal choice when replying. To identify your options within a dialogue and act accordingly to defuse rather than inflame, advise rather than dictate or deflect rather than confront is a powerful tool to be in possession of. What you say is, of course, important, but the extent to which you choose to listen will directly affect the choices you make when replying. Ignoring the words of others in order to make your point will detract from the effectiveness of the idea you are so eager to get out into the world. By not listening carefully and constructively, you could also be opening yourself up to accusations of aloofness and carelessness, and that's before you come to the realisation that you exist in an echo chamber of your own thoughts.

The sheer power of a conversation and the importance of listening was cast into the greatest relief for me by the three individuals in Part 3, who had used their words carefully to help create commonality where division, fear, rancour and hatred had existed previously. A president, a film-maker and a police officer had seen beyond the labels attached to their perceived foes to try to understand what fuelled their actions. Documentary film-maker Deeyah Khan explained to me that she had to move beyond seeing the neo-Nazis she went to film as being wholly defined by their adoption of a doctrine based on hatred, supremacy and separation – not a set of beliefs that it is easy to look beyond. She had to persuade herself that the views they exhibited weren't the entirety of who they were as people.

In exploring their lives rather than stopping at their political beliefs, she made some progress. Many remained bigoted and unrepentant, but filmed and behind-the-camera encounters with Deeyah led some to question and change beliefs that were once unassailable.

We fall out with people, we experience betrayal and acrimony. Money problems, infidelity, drugs, drink and prejudice all feed division within friendship groups, families and between communities. Former president of Ireland Mary McAleese used the principle of neighbourliness to help overcome the consequences of communal hatred. I do not wish to oversimplify a process that was years in the making and encountered many dead ends along the way, but it is worth remembering the lengths that many on both sides of the divide went to in order to build trust. That trust was built through conversation and, as fragile as it often seems, the people north and south of the border would not be where they are today without the hard work of those who knew how important it was to talk to each other.

I want us all to be reminded of how much can be achieved through talking and listening. As a police crisis negotiator, John Sutherland introduced me to the Chinese symbol for listening, 'ting'. It is the clearest representation that I have seen of what listening needs to be if it is to be truly helpful. For the Chinese, listening needed to incorporate not just the ears to hear, but the mind to think, the heart to feel and the eyes to see. Bonding these four elements together is the concept of giving the speaker your undivided attention throughout. This ancient symbol encapsulates an aspiration of how we should approach our daily interactions with others. More than any other principle in this book, it is the one I implore you to look over again and equip yourself with it. For John Sutherland, a failure to hear, see, feel, think and connect could have fatal consequences for the hostage-taker, hostage and potentially anyone within the vicinity. For you, taking on board the implications of this symbol may just result in bringing someone closer to you, building your reserves of empathy or making someone in your sphere of influence feel heard and understood.

There are no downsides to being a better listener. I often advise people who are starting out in the media to listen more than they speak and ask questions more than they make statements. Nerves, coupled with a desire to impress, can make you feel as though you must fill the space with an impressive observation or groundbreaking suggestion. When I spoke to the businessman Rick Haythornthwaite, I realised that we must continue to abide by this advice throughout life. Even if you reach the very top of an organisation, a belief that you no longer need to listen to those around you is the death knell of creativity and effectiveness. Experience and success give a person of Rick's standing the right to make decisions, but they are never made in a vacuum and understanding the role that effective dialogue plays in choosing the right course of action is essential. From the living room to the boardroom, this is a principle that we can and must aspire to.

Leadership carries with it the burden of responsibility but also the opportunity to help shape people's lives – not through moulding them into an image of your own definition but through helping someone realise what is possible and using that as a jumping-off point to explore a brave new world. This can only be done through having conversations: high-quality, well-defined conversations.

The ideas trumpeted throughout these pages boil down to very few actual core principles. Namely, that we need to recognise the value of having conversations, set about working at being better at conducting them and prevent the apps contained with our phones to override the benefit of in-person interaction. I make no apologies for wanting to drum the point home. This is a self-help book in the most literal sense, in so far as I am going to employ that which I have learned to help better prepare myself to have better conversations, as much as to inform you.

We have choices to make about the future of conversation. I cannot foresee a time where our need to connect through the spoken word will be an entirely outdated concept. I want us to create a healthier relationship with technology, whereby we actively control our access to it and ration our time locked into a virtual world so as to find space for moments in the physical one. It horrifies me to see whole families staring at screens rather than speaking to each other. A heated debate or the enlightening effect of a thoroughly good conversation cannot be replaced by a line of emojis, GIFs, memes and fifteen-second digital dopamine hits. Why can't we hand over a proportion of the academic week to learn about the benefits of verbal communication? Imagine a teacher standing before a class to break down the principles of effective social interaction and then inviting the students to practise the skills needed to be able to fully take advantage of what such an exchange creates. To repeat Professor Tanya Byron's point, we must make sure that our education system encourages rather than diminishes curiosity. The curious may well dive into the online world to find answers to the questions they have, but they will also wish to discuss those answers, refine them and even have them changed by new advice or evidence. The curious will have their ears open to empathise with the experiences of others or to process and push back on opinions they do not agree with. The curious will talk to strangers.

I always feel that pessimism is a luxury propagated by those who feel themselves sufficiently distanced from the problem so as to be unaffected by it. They display their negative outlook in the full knowledge that the issue will have no material impact on them. That is why I am an optimist. I live within this issue and know that it is well within our power to pause, reset and carry on in a different vein. If this book has served its purpose, then you will too.

As of tomorrow, be more conscious of how you communicate with others but also be mindful of how those around you behave in this regard. Don't be drawn into unnecessary arguments, whether they be online or on your high street. Refrain from being abusive and reacting abusively when provoked to do so. Realise that your worth is not defined purely by what you say but in how well you listen and connect. Alongside wanting a better body, a nicer car, a bigger house and more respectful children, why not try aspiring to have better conversations? Who knows, maybe all the other things you desire may follow shortly afterwards. Although don't hold your breath for the respectful children.

ACKNOWLEDGEMENTS

If you are about to read this final section of the book you are either a superfan or an insomniac. Long before I became the broadcaster I am today, George Mann saw something in me and asked me to present the BBC Asian Network's phone-in show. It was the making of me.

We had a fractious relationship at times, but I will never forget him showing faith in me. Alongside George was Bill Mostyn, Sej Asar, Kirren Rathor and Reva Sharma who formed the core team. They are all brilliant people to work with.

Once I left the Asian Network and joined BBC Radio 5Live, the support of the then controller Jono Wall was transformative. Without him I would not have my own mainstream radio show. Also thank you to Heidi Dawson who now heads up 5 Live and the irrepressible Julie Cullen.

Let's Talk wouldn't be half the book it is without the invaluable insights of my all-star cast of interviewees who kindly offered me their time and wisdom for this book. In order of appearance, a huge thank you to: Henry Hitchings, Johann Hari, Professor Elizabeth Stokoe, Mary McAleese, Deeyah Khan, John Sutherland, Rick Haythornthwaite, Matthew Syed, Professor Tanya Byron and Lorraine Kelly. You've taught me to be a better conversationalist.

The writing of this book would not have been possible without a group of people who had to have deep reserves of patience to work with me. These are the ones who gently cajoled me to meet deadlines that I never had any intention of meeting until I absolutely had to and pretended to believe me when I was blatantly lying to them about word counts and general progress. The first of these people is Shyam Kumar. There were other publishers who wanted to make this book with me, but I chose Trapeze because of Shyam. Throughout the excruciating process of wondering where I was at with the interviews, content, and direction of travel, his calm authoritative and guiding voice helped me to eventually plant my flag atop the mountain of creativity that is this book. His initial edit was masterful, even the butchering of my ridiculously bloated intro from ten thousand words (who writes a ten thousand word intro?!) down to a much more readable two and a half thousand.

Alongside Shyam was my literary agent Nick Walters from David Luxton Associates. His equally Zen-like approach to gently guiding me towards a completion date was invaluable. As a fellow Tottenham Hotspur fan Nick is well aware of the phrase "it's the hope that kills you." I wonder if he ever wavered in his hope that I would eventually finish *Let's talk*.

I never met or spoke to Liz Marvin, but her copyedit made the book leaner, more lucid and eminently more readable. Her side notes were succinct, bordering on brusque, but after I accepted that most of her suggestions would make the book much better, my fragile ego stepped aside so that I could embrace this vital part of the process.

Overseeing everything and helping me to realise that I had a book within me in the first place was my superstar of an agent Emily Rees Jones at M&C Saatchi Merlin. She has always believed in me, even when on occasion I haven't. She is without question the best agent that I have ever had.

A huge thankyou goes out to Shivani Ghai and Ty Keogh for allowing me to finesse the text at their beautiful house in Cape Town. It was supposed to be a family holiday, but the edits came thick and fast and their wonderful home provided me with a perfect spot to decompress whilst facing the closing stages with a calmness of mind.

Thank you to Georgia Noutsi, Nadia Assi and Anita Borvankar from Montblanc who have been so supportive of my creative endeavours. The notes of every interview I do are written down with a Montblanc Meisterstuck ballpoint: it is my lightsaber.

My publishers, Trapeze, are part of Orion and having Francesca Pearce on my side when it comes to publicity has been an absolute gift. She is one of the very best. Alongside publicity comes marketing and I would also like to thank Katie Moss for being part of a brilliant team.

After months of trying and failing to write at home I then decamped to a super-cool eatery called Aunty Ji's in Manchester. Sadly, the food was too distracting and I ate more than I wrote. Perhaps due to my expanding waistline I discovered that it was my local David Lloyd gym that proved to be the best place to write. As men and women spray painted in Lycra strutted past, I went through litres of oat milk matcha lattes, with Montblanc headphones clamped to my head listening to the beautiful music of Ludovico Einaudi on repeat. The words began to flow – much to the relief of Shyam, Nick and all involved.

Thank you to the Festive Boys and Simon Gone But Not Forgotten WhatsApp groups which are made up of some of the most inspirational men in my life. Shout out to Oli Spencer for keeping me stylish and being a true friend. I speak to Terry Betts and Andy Holland almost every day. Thank you for always being there for me. I am a fragile chap. Your friendship keeps me intact. As does the lifelong friendship of Jason Abbey. Also, I want to send a massive shout to my brother Rohan Arthanayake, sister-in-law Rachita and nephew Charles.

Lastly, I would like you, the reader, to know that everything I do is fortified by the love I have for Eesha Arthanayake, and our children Aarya and Kingsley. They uplift, infuriate, inspire and challenge me in ways that constantly surprise me. I hope they never forget that as far as the world knows we are "a normal family."

SELECTED BIBLIOGRAPHY
BY CHAPTER

1: Let's Talk About History
Everett, Daniel, *How Language Began: The Story of Humanity's Greatest Achievement* (Profile Books, 2017)
Boë, J-L., Sawallis, T. R., Fagot, J., Badin, P., Barbier, G., Captier, G., Ménard, L., Heim, J-L., Schwartz, J-L. (2019), 'Which way to the dawn of speech?: Reanalyzing half a century of debates and data in light of speech science', *Science Advances*, Vol. 5, No. 12
Xenophon, trans. Dakyns, H. G., *Symposium* www.gutenberg.org/files/1181/1181-h/1181-h.htm
Aelfric of Eynsham, *Colloquy*

2: Henry Hitchings: The Growth of Conversation
Hitchings, Henry, *Dr Johnson's Dictionary* (John Murray, 2005)
Congreve, William, *The Way of the World* (1700) in *The*

Way of the World and Other Plays (Penguin Classics, 2006)

3: *Johann Hari Conversation and the Attention Crisis*
Hari, Johann, *Stolen Focus: Why You Can't Pay Attention* (Bloomsbury, 2022)
Dweck, Carol, *Mindset: Changing The Way You think To Fulfil Your Potential* (updated edition) (Robinson, 2017)
Hari, Johann, *Chasing the Scream* (Bloomsbury, 2019)
Sullivan, Andrew, 'Here Comes the Groom: A (conservative) case for gay marriage', *New Republic*, 28 August 1989 newrepublic.com/article/79054/ here-comes-the-groom
Sullivan, Andrew, *Virtually Normal: An Argument about Homosexuality* (Picador, 1995)

4: *Let's Talk About Talking*
Turkle, Sherry, *The Second Self: Computers and the Human Spirit* (MIT Press, 1985)
Teo, Alan R., Choi, Hwajung, Valenstein, Marcia (2013), 'Social relationships and depression: ten-year follow-up from a nationally representative study', PLoS One, 30;8(4)
Making Caring Common Project, 'Loneliness in America: How the Pandemic Has Deepened an Epidemic of Loneliness and What We Can Do About It', Harvard Graduate School of Education, February 2021
Turkle, Sherry, *Reclaiming Conversation: The Power of*

Talk in a Digital Age (Penguin Press, 2015)

Przybylski, Andrew K., Weinstein, Netta (2012), 'Can you connect with me now? How the presence of mobile communication technology influences face-to-face conversation quality', Journal of Social and Personal Relationships, Vol. 30, Iss. 3

Seltzer, Leslie J., Prososki, Ashley R., Ziegler, Toni E., Pollak, Seth D. (2012), 'Instant Messages vs speech: hormones and why we still need to hear each other', *Evolution of Human Behaviour*, Vol. 33, Iss. 1

5: Professor Elizabeth Stokoe The Structure of a Conversation

Speer, Susan A., Stokoe, Elizabeth, *Conversation and Gender* (Cambridge University Press, 2011)

Stokoe, Elizabeth, *Talk: The Science of Conversation* (Robinson, 2020)

Sikveland, Rein Ove, Kevoe-Feldman, Heidi, Stokoe, Elizabeth, *Crisis Talk: Negotiating with Individuals in Crisis* (Routledge, 2022)

7: Mary McAleese Drawing Paramilitaries into the Peace Process

McAleese, Mary, *Here's the Story* (Penguin Ireland, 2020)

9: John Sutherland Lessons from a Hostage Negotiator

Sutherland, John, *Blue: A Memoir – Keeping the Peace and Falling to Pieces* (Weidenfeld and Nicolson, 2018)

274

Glover, Stephen, 'Yes he was armed, drunk and deranged. But wasn't it overkill for seven officers to shoot dead Mark Saunders?' *Daily Mail*, 30 September 2010

10: *Let's Talk About Jobs*
Office for National Statistics, 'Business and individual attitudes towards the future of homeworking, UK: April to May 2021', 14 June 2021
Van Bommel, Tara (2021), 'Remote-Work Options Can Boost Productivity and Curb Burnout', Catalyst
Grenny, Joseph, Maxfield, David, 'A Study of 1,100 Employees Found That Remote Workers Feel Shunned and Left Out', *Harvard Business Review*, 2 November 2017

12: *Matthew Syed Hierarchies in Business*
Syed, Matthew, *Bounce: The of Myth of Talent and the Power of Practice* (Fourth Estate, 2011)
Syed, Matthew, *Black Box Thinking* (John Murray, 2015)
Syed, Matthew, *Rebel Ideas: The Power of Diverse Thinking* (John Murray, 2019)

13: *Let's Talk About Interviews*
Peterson, Jordan B., *12 Rules for Life: An Antidote to Chaos* (Allen Lane, 2018)

14: How to be More Curious
Kelly, Lorraine, *Shine: Discover a Brighter You* (Century, 2019)

Conclusion
Miller, Stephen, *Conversation: A History of a Declining Art* (Yale University Press, 2006)